I Love Letters!

by Jean Feldman and Holly Karapetkova

I Love Letters!

by Jean Feldman and Holly Karapetkova

Additional Gryphon House Books Written by Jean Feldman:

Rainy Day Activities

Transition Time

Transition Tips and Tricks

I Love Letters!

More Than 200 Quick & Easy Activities to Introduce Young Children to Letters and Literacy

Jean Feldman and
Holly Karapetkova
Illustrated by
Deborah Johnson

Gryphon House, Inc.
Lewisville, NC

© 2009 Jean Feldman and Holly Karapetkova
Published by Gryphon House, Inc.
PO Box 10, Lewisville, NC 27023
800.638.0928 (toll free); 877.638.7576 (fax)

Visit us on the web at www.gryphonhouse.com

Illustrations: Deborah Johnson

Cover Art: Stock Xpert (Image #id8333792), www.stockxpert.com; Child Photograph: Straight Shots Photography, Ellicott City, Maryland ©2006.

Reprinted June 2012

Library of Congress Cataloging-in-Publication Information

Feldman, Jean R.
 I love letters / by Jean Feldman and Holly Karapetkova.
   p. cm.
 ISBN 978-0-87659-080-5
 1. English language--Alphabet--Study and teaching (Early childhood)--Activity programs. 2. Language arts (Early childhood)--Activity
programs. I. Karapetkova, Holly. II. Title.
  LB1525.65.J43 2009
  372.46'5--dc22

                    2008030357

Table of Contents

Chapter 6: Feel! Taste! Touch!: Multi-Sensory Materials to Activate Senses and Engage Children in Hands-on Learning..................................73

Chapter 7: Letter Games: Games That Teach! 83

Chapter 8: Write On! Pre-Writing Experiences to Get Children Ready to Write 93

Chapter 9: Letters to Send Home: Strategies to Involve Families 113

Appendix..............................129

Index 139

Preface

If you were not an educator, and you wanted to get your child ready to read, what skills do you think she would need? What things would you try to teach her to help her on her way? Common sense would suggest letters! Those 26 little letters are where it all begins! They are the tools of a reader—little wiggles and squiggles that turn into words, stories, poems, and great literature. Letters are an integral part of our environment. From the clothes we wear, to the food we eat, to the signs on the road, it's a letter world! Children are naturally curious about letters and will be excited about learning them when they are introduced in a multi-sensory, playful way. No workbooks! No worksheets! No drill and kill! We need to create activities and experiences where children—all children—will succeed as they become acquainted with those 26 "friends" that will open the door to reading, writing, and a lifetime of learning!

It has been frustrating over the years to see the pendulum of early childhood education swing back and forth in debates on when and how letters should be introduced. One extreme warns, "Don't teach letters to young children at all. Don't even display alphabet letters in your classroom." On the other end of the continuum are those who endorse phonics workbooks and formal writing instruction for the youngest of children. In truth, recent research has validated the importance of developing alphabet knowledge in the preschool years. Letters are not "good," "bad," "right," or "wrong." It's the way we introduce them and reinforce them that needs to be carefully examined.

Language is not a simple skill, and the pathways in the brain that control language ability connect and overlap in complicated ways. The more diverse and fun methods we can use to get kids to look at letters, the more likely those letters will "stick" in their brains, and the more likely they will become avid and successful readers. Don't be afraid to introduce these concepts even if you feel they are "above" the current ability of some of your students. We read to even the smallest children;

we give toddlers letter blocks and other letter toys to play with, though we hardly expect them to know the difference between A and Z. The key is to nurture an excitement for letters and a love for learning that will stay with students throughout their lives.

Whenever I have the opportunity to sing letter songs with children, I get very excited as I say, "I love letters. Do you?" (A few children will raise their hands with this question.) And then I add, "Smart people love letters. Do you?" You should see the hands shoot up! Everybody wants to be smart! You see, teachers have to be salespeople. We have to "sell" our product (letters) to our students! With technology and all the games and media that we have to compete with, we must rise to the challenge and create activities that will spark children's creativity, motivate them, and sustain their interest!

There are many ways to make chocolate chip cookies, and do you know what? They all turn out yummy! This book is like a cookbook with more than 100 activities and ideas for nurturing literacy and a love of reading. Choose, adapt, and use the ones that best meet the needs of your children and your goals.

Let's see how much fun this can be!

Dr. Jean & Dr. Holly

Introduction

Evidence-Based Reading Research (EBRR) and Brain Research:
Knowing *Why* and *How* to Do What's Best for Children

There is no definitive "right" or "wrong" way to introduce letters. Here are some suggestions from the National Association for the Education of Young Children:

"Children's proficiency in letter naming is a well-established predictor of their end-of-year achievement, probably because it mediates the ability to remember sounds. Generally a good rule according to current learning theory is to start with the more easily visualized uppercase letters, to be followed by identifying lowercase letters. In each case, introducing just a few letters at a time, rather than many, enhances mastery." (Learning to Read and Write: Developmentally Appropriate Practices, 1998)

The 2002 report by the National Early Literacy Panel found certain skills have direct links to children's eventual success in literacy development. The number one variable listed was alphabetic knowledge. They emphasized the importance of providing children with the opportunity to play with letters, link letter names and sounds, sing songs, engage in oral language activities, and draw and write independently.

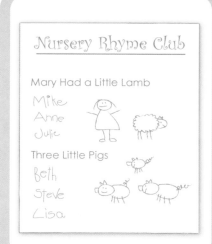

Principles from learning theory and brain research can further assist in defining meaningful alphabet activities for young children:

- Children just want to have fun! Focus on playful activities that expose children to letters, sounds, words, and books in a variety of ways.

- The more senses you activate, the more likely the message will get to the brain! Children need to see, hear, smell, taste, and touch letters.

- The brain likes novelty and challenges. It's got to be new and exciting to capture children's attention.

"Y" is for Yolonda!

- Repetition with feedback is important. Children need to do things over and over again, but they must do it correctly with coaching to fully benefit them.

- We remember things as a whole. Therefore, expose children to all the letters through songs and books. Then focus more intensely on specific letters using children's names, common themes, and topics of interest.

- Prior learning is important. If children know a little bit about something, then it's easier for them to grasp the concept when formally presented. ABC books, rhymes, toys, and games are powerful ways to expose children to letters and sounds.

- The brain loves music and movement. Songs are the most "convenient" way to learn anything!

- Learning must be connected to previous experiences if it is to be meaningful. Teaching children to memorize the ABCs without integrating the alphabet within the context of the curriculum and their lives is a moot point.

- Learning proceeds from simple to complex and from large to small. Build on children's successes in small incremental steps.

- Every brain is unique. No two children learn in the same way or at the same time. Therefore, it is important to be sensitive to children's individual styles, and to provide them with a wide variety of opportunities to learn, play, and interact with letters and language.

Correlations of Preschool Skills or Abilities with Decoding or
Reading Comprehension Measures
Educational Leadership, March, 2004 (74–77)

Decoding or Reading Comprehension Measures

Alphabetic Knowledge

Print Knowledge

Environmental Print

Invented Spelling

Listening Comprehension

Oral Language/Vocabulary

Phonemic Awareness

Phonological Short-Term Memory

Rapid Naming

Visual Memory

Visual Perceptual Skills

Preschool Skills or Abilities Related to Decoding or Reading
Comprehension Measures

Alphabetic Knowledge

Play with letters

Link the names of letters and the sounds

Work with rhymes and play language games

Draw and write independently for personal enjoyment

Print Knowledge

Observe adults writing as they say the words aloud

Contribute ideas for others to write down

Participate in discussions about labels and signs

Observe and follow along as adults track print from left to right

Independently look at books and draw and "write"

Oral Language

Create sounds by singing and participating in music making

Listen and respond to music, stories, and discussions

Listen for various purposes: for enjoyment, to follow directions,
    to engage in dialogue, and to attend to patterns in language

Engage in oral language activities that are verbally stimulating

CHAPTER 1

Print Knowledge: Creating a Print-Rich Environment

Creating a Literate Environment

Before children read words, they "read" pictures. By looking at pictures and words together, children will begin to make print connections. Remember that children are not expected to be reading yet when you begin these activities. The important thing is to model and validate that reading and writing are useful and fun! Your mission is to help children believe that they are readers and writers.

Skill Development

Children will:

- connect spoken word with print
- develop small motor skills
- integrate reading and writing
- develop alphabet knowledge
- see the importance of reading and writing
- use oral language

Create a literate environment using the following ideas:

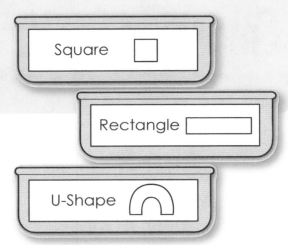

Labels and Signs

Make meaningful labels with pictures so children know where to store toys and classroom materials. Use pictures of objects from school catalogs, pictures from the boxes the toys come from, or take digital pictures. You might start the year with the word and picture, and then later in the year use a sentence with the picture.

Sign-In Chart

Make a sign-in chart using a large sheet of paper or a section of your chalkboard. Have the children sign their names when they enter the classroom every day. Explain, "It's important for me to know that you are here, so be sure and sign in!" Encourage scribbles, pictures, or any marks they put on the paper.

■ ■ ■ ■ ■ ■

Hint! Place name cards near the sign-in chart so when children are ready to write their names, they can use the cards as models.

Daily Schedule

Write your daily schedule on a poster board and illustrate it with classroom photos or pictures from school catalogs. Review the schedule every day in sequential order. Ask questions, such as, "What are we going to do after music?" When children respond, ask, "How did you know that?" When they explain that they looked at the picture, reinforce with, "That's what readers do!"

Hint! Write different events on index cards and attach a piece of magnetic tape to the back of each card. This allows you to change the schedule easily when your routine varies.

Morning Message

Before children arrive at school, write a message to them about special events that will happen that day on a language experience chart. At Circle Time, read over the message, tracking from left to right. Have children point out letters or words that they recognize. This activity not only creates positive feelings about the day, but is a personal way to reinforce reading and writing skills.

Hint! You might want a class mascot (puppet or stuffed animal) to present the morning message.

Taking Turns

Keep a clipboard or dry-erase board next to popular centers, such as the Block Center or Home Living Area. Children "sign up" (make a mark) for a turn. Show them how to cross through their names to indicate they have had a turn. You could also use a list for taking home a favorite book, sitting next to you (or other favored adult) at lunch, or for having a turn on a piece of playground equipment.

Pocket Chart

Write words to poems or nursery rhymes on sentence strips and put them in a pocket chart. Track the words as you say the rhyme out loud. Let the children take turns pointing to the words. Mix up the lines and have children come up and unscramble them.

- Write the title and draw a picture clue of different songs and fingerplays that children enjoy. Place these in a pocket chart. When you have a few extra minutes, let children select their favorite one.

- Write the words to the "Happy Birthday" song on sentence strips and cut out each word. The birthday child gets to scramble the words on each line and then the class has to sing the silly version. (The children think this is hilarious!)

Language Experience Chart

Keep a large chart tablet in the front of the classroom and use it for making lists, brainstorming, dictation, writing reminders, reviewing events at the end of the day, and so on.

Poems and Songs

Write words to poems, songs, and fingerplays on posters and follow along as you sing and chant.

Take two crackers.

Spread one cracker with cheese spread.

Put the second cracker on top of first cracker.

Eat.

Rebus Charts

Make picture charts for centers so children can follow directions to make a recipe, do art projects, perform science experiments, and so on.

Message Center

Provide a dry-erase board or chalkboard where children can write notes to each other. Children will also enjoy writing sticky notes and posting them around the room.

Mirror Messages

Write notes on a classroom mirror using a dry-erase marker. You could write a birthday message, word, reminder, or special accomplishment.

Functional Books

You can make functional books using spiral notebooks, composition books, or by stapling paper together. Use them for celebrating birthdays, teaching the children their phone numbers, and many other daily events (see the following suggestions). These books help children understand that reading and writing are meaningful and useful in our daily lives.

Skill Development

Children will:

- develop print knowledge
- integrate reading and writing
- develop social skills
- gain motivation to read and write

Things the Teacher Needs to Know

Write "Things the Teacher Needs to Know" on the front of a composition book or spiral notebook. Explain to the children that you don't always have time to listen to everything they want to tell you, but you are very interested in what they want to share. Show them the special notebook and tell them they can write down their concerns when you are busy helping another child or working on a task. When a child comes to you to ask or tell you something and you cannot give the child your full attention, hand him the book and say, "Write it all down and don't leave out a thing. I'll read it later on when I have more time." The child can draw a picture and scribble his "message." Make sure to respond to the child's page as soon as possible so he knows his thoughts are important.

Classroom Rule Book

After discussing school and classroom rules, ask each child to come up with a rule that he thinks is important. Each child illustrates his rule and writes or dictates a sentence to go with it. Put the children's "rule" pages together to make a class book. Place the book in a prominent spot in your classroom and refer to it when children are behaving inappropriately. You might say, "Children, please walk (or fill in appropriate behavior). It's one of our classroom rules; it even says so right here in our book!"

New or Favorite Shoes Book

Staple blank white paper in between construction paper to make a book. Draw a pair of shoes on the front and write "New or Favorite Shoe Book." When children get a new pair of shoes, sing this song to the tune of "This Old Man." Because some children may not get new shoes often (or at all), encourage all the children to also sing and write about their favorite shoes.

> *Here's one foot.*
> *Here are two.*
> *Each is wearing a brand new shoe. (OR Each has on a favorite shoe.)*
> *So stand up, turn around, dance around the floor.*
> *That's what these new shoes are for!*

Invite children to write a story or draw a picture of their shoes on one of the pages of the book.

Weather Report

Punch holes in the left side of blank paper and put the pages in a pocket folder. Write "What's the Weather?" on the front and decorate with a sun, umbrella, cloud, and other weather symbols. Choose a different child each day to be the "meteorologist." Sing a song about the weather, similar to the one below, and ask the meteorologist to record the weather in the book.

> **(Tune: "Shortnin' Bread")**
> *What will the weather, weather, weather,*
> *What will the weather be today?*
> *It is* [sunny, sunny, sunny]. (meteorologist inserts the appropriate word for the day's weather)
> *It is* [sunny, sunny] *today.*

Class Birthday Book

Cover two 9" x 12" pieces of cardboard with wrapping paper to make a cover for this book. Insert blank paper, hole punch, and bind with book rings. When a child has a birthday, take a photo of him and encourage him to dictate or write a story about his special day.

Individual Birthday Books

This book makes a great gift for each child in the class on his birthday. When a child celebrates a birthday, cut the front and back off a gift bag. Cut paper to match the dimensions of the gift bag and give a sheet to each child in the class. Each child draws a picture of a birthday wish he would give his friend. After children present their pictures to the birthday child, staple the pages between the front and the back of the gift bag to make a book.

Acts of Kindness

Brainstorm what acts of kindness are. Use a small spiral notebook to make a class "Acts of Kindness" book. Tell the children that when a classmate does something to help them or does another kind deed, they can record it in the notebook by drawing a picture or dictating a sentence about it for you to write.

Hint! Model acts of kindness by "catching children" in the act of doing something kind for others. You might say, "I want to write this down in the book so I don't forget it!"

Class Phone Book

Give the children paper and ask them to write their names at the top and their "phone numbers" at the bottom (pretend numbers are fine!). Younger children can scribble their names and numbers. Take a photo of each child and glue it to the middle of the child's page. To make a cover for your book, cut the front and back covers off of an old local phone book. Punch holes and bind with book rings. Place this in the Home Living Area next to a play phone or old cell phone.

Forms

Create forms for children to fill out with their name, date of birth, eye color, hair color, address, phone number, and so on. Pretend numbers and addresses are fine for children to use. (Vary according to their ability.) You could use these to make pretend driver's licenses, credit cards, library cards, and so on.

Environmental Print

When children pick out their favorite box of cereal, recognize a stop sign, or point out a favorite restaurant, they are reading! Environmental print includes signs, symbols, and logos that children see everywhere and every day in their environment. It is a natural way to help children make print connections and capture their interest.

Skill Development

Children will:

- gain print knowledge
- make a connection between the real world and school
- improve visual memory
- practice visual discrimination

School Supply Catalogs

Use pictures from school supply catalogs to make classroom labels and center signs.

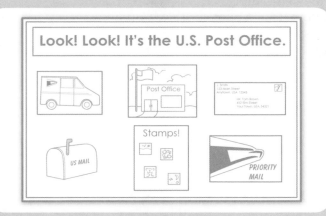

Photos from School and Community

Take pictures around your school and community and use them for a bulletin board display or a classroom book. For example, make a post office display titled: "Look! Look! It's the U.S. Post Office." Hang photos of mail trucks, mail carriers, mailboxes, letters, stamps, and the post office. Add appropriate text, especially real-life examples of post office items.

Hint! This would be a great project to send home for children to fill in with their parents.

I Can Read!

Make a blank book for each child by stapling white paper together or punching holes into paper and binding it together with yarn or rings. Invite the children to cut out words they can read and glue them on the pages.

Old Mother Hubbard

Draw a picture of a cupboard on a sheet of construction paper and use it for the cover of your book. Ask children to bring in wrappers from favorite foods. At the top of each page write:

Old Mother Hubbard went to her cupboard
To get her poor dog a bone.
But when she got there the cupboard was bare
And so the poor dog had _____.

Let children glue their wrappers under the rhyme and then "read" the word.

Pictures, Letters, and Words

Use environmental print to help children differentiate between pictures, letters, and words. Fold a sheet of paper into a brochure (tri-fold). Have the children cut out pictures, letters, and words from old magazines and newspapers. Ask them to glue the pictures in the first section of the "brochure," letters in the second section, and words in the third section.

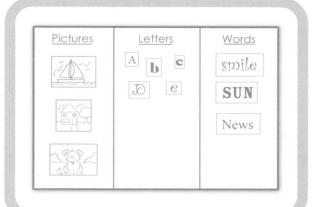

Coupons

Bring in the coupon circulars from the Sunday paper and let the children cut out the coupons. Have them sort the coupons (by type of product, amount of savings, and so on) in the Math Center and then use them for play in the Home Living Area.

I Like...

Provide cereal boxes, snack food containers, yogurt containers, and containers from other favorite children's food. Help children cut out labels from the containers of food they like. Write "I" on one index card and "like" on another index card for each child. Children spread out the cards and add food labels

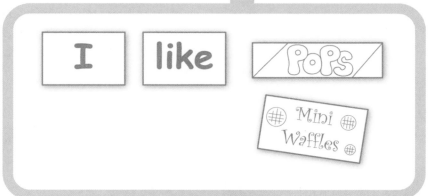

as they make sentences that they can read. For example: "I like goldfish crackers." Attach magnetic tape to the back of the cards and logos for children to use at home on their refrigerators.

Signs

Make traffic signs for the Block Center. Attach signs to paper towel rolls so they will stand up.

Clothes

Read the labels on clothes children wear to school, such as T-shirts, athletic shoes, jackets, and so on.

Walk and Read

Walk around the school with the children and make a list of words that you see.

Newspaper

Have the children use a highlighter to find letters or words that they can read.

Food Containers for Fun

Have children save wrappers, boxes, and containers from foods and bring them in. Use them for sorting, graphing, and so on. Put prices on the containers, place them in the Home Living Area, and encourage children to buy items with play money.

Take-Out Bags

Collect clean bags from restaurants and grocery stores. Punch a hole in the upper left corner of each bag and bind with a book ring. Flip through the bags as children "read" the logos.

Box Tops

Recycle food boxes children bring in from home with some of these games.

- **Matching:** Cut the fronts and backs off boxes. Mix them up and challenge the children to match the ones that go together. Start with four pairs and increase the number when appropriate.

- **Concentration**: Place the fronts and backs of the boxes face down on the floor. Turn over two at a time and play a memory game. Again, start with four pairs and increase the difficulty.

- **Label Match**: Cut the top section with the label off the boxes. Children try to match up the labels with the correct food box.

- **Sewing Cards**: Punch holes around the sides of box tops. Children sew through the holes with yarn (wrapped with tape at one end) or shoelaces.

- **Books**: Make a book called "What's for Breakfast?" Ask the children to bring in an empty box from their favorite cereal. Help the children cut off the front of the box. Write a sentence on a strip of paper using the child's name (for example, "Lucy eats Oaties"). Have the child glue the sentence to his box. Punch holes into all the box tops and bind with book rings.

- **Puzzles**: Cut box tops into puzzle shapes. Store in a resealable bag. Older children will enjoy making these themselves, and the cutting will provide additional fine motor practice for them.

- **Fractions**: Invite children to cut box tops in half, fourths, and eighths. Talk about the different fractions with the children and have them put the halves, fourths, and eighths back together so they can see that all the parts make a whole.

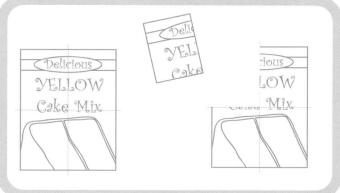

Oral Language

Oral Language

Oral language is the foundation of literacy and is key to intellectual, social, and emotional development. *Expressive language* refers to speaking and writing; *receptive language* includes listening and reading. Language develops naturally as children listen to and imitate others. Language growth is dramatic in children's first five years; this is when they learn the basic patterns of speech they will need for all future communication.

You can foster language development by modeling appropriate language. Encourage the children to talk, sing, and chant, and provide opportunities where they can interact socially with friends. Remember, a noisy classroom is one where children are developing a foundation for literacy! It is also important to listen, using your eyes, smile, and body language, when young children speak.

Skill Development

Children will:

- use oral language
- increase auditory memory
- practice eye-hand coordination

Nurture children's oral language using the following ideas:

Routines

- Greet children each day with a song or special rhyme. For example, sing the following song to the tune of "Skip to My Lou":

  Hello, (child's name), how are you? (class sings)
  Hello, (child's name), how are you?
  Hello, (child's name), how are you?
  I am fine, and I hope you are, too! (child answers)

- Have a "compliment circle" and invite children to go around the circle and make positive comments about each classmate.

- Say the following chant to end your day:

  Hey, hey, what do say?
  What did you learn in school today?
  (The children take turns saying what they learned or liked best.)

Model Language

Encourage children to answer questions in complete sentences. Instead of correcting them, model the way you would like them to answer. They can echo your response.

Microphone

Purchase a play microphone or make one by wrapping aluminum foil around a paper towel roll. Invite the children to pass around the microphone and take turns speaking into it.

■ ■ ■ ■ ■ ■ ■ ■
Hint! Put a round sticker on the microphone and call it the "volume" button. If they use a soft voice, ask them to "turn up the volume." If they are too loud, ask them to "turn it down."

Partner Share

Have children choose partners. Have the pairs tell each other about their favorite part of the day, a favorite story or hobby, their families, and other topics.

Happy Bag

Decorate a cloth bag and write "Happy Bag" on it. Let a different child each day take the bag home and put a special object in it. Add a note for families to help their children write three clues about what is in the bag or use the rhyme below:

> I don't mean to brag,
> But I have something in my bag.
> If you listen to my clue,
> I bet you can guess it, too.
> It rhymes with_____.

Photos

Although "A picture is worth a thousand words," children will be eager to discuss photos you take of them at school. They will also enjoy bringing pictures from home and talking about their families and experiences.

Echo Game

Begin the game by cupping your hands around your mouth and saying, "Yoohoo." Children repeat, "Yoohoo." Then say another word or phrase. Children listen and echo it back. After you model this a few times, let the children take turns saying a word or phrase that their classmates echo back.

Stretch out sounds in words and ask children to blend the sounds and identify the words.

Children's Rhymes and Games

Familiar jump rope rhymes and children's games, such as "Mother May I?" and "Simon Says" are fun for language development.

Missing Word

As you say rhymes or read books, stop and encourage children to fill in the missing word.

Hint! Check out kididdles.com for some great rhymes!

Rhymes to Read

Through repetition of nursery rhymes, fingerplays, and poems, children develop important concepts about print as well as left-to-right orientation. Write popular poems and rhymes on a language experience chart, poster, overhead projector, or pocket chart and track the words with your finger or pointer as you read. You can also photocopy poems and glue them onto index cards. Keep them on a book ring or in your pocket to use for a "brain break" or to focus children's attention during transitions.

For example, write the nursery rhyme "Humpty Dumpty" on a poster. The children say the rhyme as you point to each word. Next, clap out the beat of the rhyme. Have the children stand up and jump on each syllable. Ask them questions. "Do you hear any words that rhyme? Look at the words *wall* and *fall*. Do you notice anything similar about the words? Do you know other words that sound like *wall*? What letter does Humpty's name start with? What sound does that letter make? Is there anything in our classroom that starts with that sound?"

Skill Development

Children will:

- practice oral language
- increase phonological awareness
- improve auditory memory

Use some of the following rhymes, fingerplays, and poems:

Grandma's Glasses (traditional)
These are grandma's glasses. (make circles around eyes)
This is grandma's hat. (cup hands and place on head)
And this is the way
She folds her hands (fold hands and put in your lap)
And puts them in her lap.

These are grandpa's glasses. (make circles around eyes
   and talk in a deep voice)
This is grandpa's hat. (cup hands and place on head)
And this is the way
He folds his arms (cross arms and fold)
Just like that!

Teddy Bear (traditional)

Teddy bear, teddy bear,
Turn around. (turn around)
Teddy bear, teddy bear,
Touch the ground. (touch the ground)
Teddy bear, teddy bear,
Read the news. (pretend to read)
Teddy bear, teddy bear,
Tie your shoes. (bend down to shoes)
Teddy bear, teddy bear,
Go upstairs. (pretend to climb stairs)
Teddy bear, teddy bear,
Say your prayers. (fold hands)
Teddy bear, teddy bear,
Turn off the light. (pretend to touch light switch)
Teddy bear, teddy bear,
Say, "Good night." (place head on hands and close eyes)

Here Is a Bunny (traditional)

Here is a bunny (hold up two fingers)
With ears so funny.
And here's his hole in the ground. (make hole with other hand)
At the first sound he hears,
He pricks up his ears, (wiggle ears)
Then hops to his hole in the ground! (hop "bunny" into "hole")

Here Is a Turtle (traditional)

Here is a turtle. (make fist)
He lives in a shell. (stick out thumb)
He likes his home (insert thumb in fist)
Very well.
When he gets hungry (stick out thumb)
He comes out to eat.
Then he goes back into (tuck thumb back in fist)
His house to sleep.

Have a Cup of Tea (traditional)

Here's a cup. (hold up right hand)
And here's a cup. (hold left hand)
And here's a pot of tea. (put hands together)
Pour a cup. (pretend to pour in right hand)
And pour a cup. (pour in left hand)
And have a cup with me! (pretend to drink)

Me (traditional)

I've got ten little fingers
And ten little toes. (hold up hands)
Two little eyes (point to eyes)
And a mouth and a nose. (point)
Put them all together, (circle arms)
And what have you got? (hands on hips)
You've got me, baby, (put thumbs in chest)
And that's a lot! (wiggle hips)

Ten Little Friends (traditional)

Ten little friends (hold up fingers)
Went out to play (wiggle fingers)
On a very bright
And sunny day.
And they took a little walk.
Walk, walk, walk. (walk fingers in front)
And they had a little talk.
Talk, talk, talk. (put fingertips together)
They climbed up a great big hill (move fingers up in air)
And stood on the top very still.
Then they all tumbled down (roll hands around and down)
And fell to the ground.
"We're so tired," (hold up fingers)
They all said.
So they all went home
And went to bed.
10 – 9 – 8 – 7 – 6 – 5 – 4 – 3 – 2 – 1. (put down fingers one at a time)
Good night! (place head on hands)

Heidi High and Louie Low (traditional)

[Every time Heidi High speaks use a high, soft voice. Every time
Louie Low talks use a deep, loud voice. Begin by sticking up your
thumbs. Wiggle your right thumb and say in a high, soft voice, "This
is Heidi High." Wiggle your left thumb and say in a deep, loud voice,
"This is Louie Low." Tuck your thumbs in your hands and extend
them to either side of you as you begin telling the story below.]

One day Heidi High opened her door *(open fingers)*, went outside
(stick out right thumb), and closed her door *(close fingers).* She said
(wiggle right thumb), "What a beautiful day! I'm going to visit my
friend Louie Low."

So Heidi went up the hill and down the hill and up the hill and down the hill *(move right thumb up and down in front of body until it reaches your left fist)*. She knocked on the front door and said *(pretend to knock on left fist with right hand),* "Oh, Louie Low. Oh, Louie Low. Let me try the back door. *(knock on opposite side of left fist)* Oh, Louie Low. Oh, Louie Low. I guess he's not home." So Heidi went up the hill and down the hill and up the hill and down the hill *(move right thumb up and down back in front of your body)*.

When she got home, she opened her door, went inside, and shut her door *(open fingers, tuck in thumb, then close fingers to make a fist)*.

The next day Louie Low opened his door *(open fingers),* went outside *(stick out left thumb),* and closed his door *(close fingers).* He said *(wiggle left thumb),* "What a beautiful day! I'm going to go visit my friend Heidi High." [Continue same as Heidi did on the previous day.]

The next day both Heidi High and Louie Low opened their doors *(open fingers)*, went outside *(stick out thumbs),* and closed their doors *(close fingers).* Heidi said *(wiggle right thumb)*, "What a beautiful day! I'm going to go visit my friend Louie Low." And Louie said *(wiggle left thumb),* "What a beautiful day! I'm going to visit my friend Heidi High." So they both went up the hill and down the hill *(move thumbs toward each other until they meet in front of your body)* until they ran into each other. They danced and played and had the best time *(wiggle thumbs).* After a while Heidi said, "Well, Louie, I better go home." And Louie said, "Well, Heidi, I better go home." So they gave each other a hug *(hug thumbs),* and they both went up the hill and down the hill *(wiggle thumbs apart to opposite sides of the body).* When they got home they opened their doors *(open fingers),* went inside *(tuck in thumbs),* closed their doors *(close fingers),* and went to sleep *(quietly put hands together and lay your head on them).*

This Little Girl and This Little Boy (traditional)
This little girl is ready for bed. (hold up index finger and wiggle)
On the pillow she lays her head. (open palm and lay finger down)
Wrap the covers around her tight. (wrap fist around finger)
That's the way she spends the night. (rock hand)
Morning comes, she opens her eyes.
Off with a toss the covers fly. (open fist)
She jumps out of bed, (hold up finger)
Eats her breakfast, (pretend to feed)
And brushes her teeth. (pretend to brush teeth)

She gets dressed and (pretend to dress finger)
Brushes her hair. (pretend to brush hair)
Now she's ready and on her way, (dance finger around)
To work and play at school all day.

This little boy…(use the opposite index finger to do this verse)

King Kong (traditional)
[Say "King Kong" in a loud voice and "teeny tiny monkey" in a
   squeaky voice.]
King Kong (flex arms)
Was just a teeny tiny monkey (hold up pinky)
Compared to my love for you.
King Kong (flex arms)
Was just a teeny tiny monkey (hold up pinky)
Compared to my love for you.
I love you day (make sun with arms)
And night. (place head on hands)
My love is out of sight. (hands in air)
King Kong (flex arms)
Was just a teeny tiny monkey
Compared to my love for you!

Miss Molly (traditional)
Miss Molly had a dolly (cradle arms and rock)
Who was sick, sick, sick.
So she called for the doctor (pretend to hold a phone)
To come quick, quick, quick.
The doctor came (pretend to hold up bag)
With his bag and his hat. (touch head)
And he knocked on the door
With a rat-a-tat-tat. (pretend to knock)
He looked at the dolly
And he shook his head. (shake head)
He said, "Miss Molly,
Put her straight to bed." (point finger)
He wrote on some paper
For some pills, pills, pills. (pretend to write)
I'll be back in the morning
With the bills, bills, bills. (wave good-bye)

Nursery Rhymes for All Times

Children have enjoyed nursery rhymes for hundreds of years, which is certainly testimony of their appeal to children. Nursery rhymes are short, simple, and part of our literary heritage. Oral language, auditory memory, phonological awareness, and interest in print are all fostered with nursery rhymes. Best of all, they are enjoyable and can be integrated throughout the day to engage children. You can have children begin to identify characters, the setting, the problem, and resolution with traditional rhymes.

(**Note:** See pages 134–136 in the Appendix for the words to many nursery rhymes.)

Skill Development

Children will:

- practice oral language
- increase phonological awareness
- improve auditory memory
- begin forming a foundation of literacy
- start developing concepts about print

The following are some simple activities for integrating nursery rhymes daily in your classroom.

Nursery Rhyme Tunes

Sing traditional nursery rhymes to familiar tunes such as "100 Bottles of Pop on the Wall," "Yankee Doodle," "Sweet Betsy from Pike," and "What Do You Do with a Drunken Sailor?"

Story Elements

Discuss the story elements in nursery rhymes, such as characters, setting, problem, and resolution. For example, in "Little Miss Muffet," the characters are Miss Muffet and the spider, the problem is that a spider scares her when she is eating her curds and whey, and the resolution is for her to run away from the spider.

Rhyme of the Week

Select a different nursery rhyme each week and write it on a poster or language experience chart. Reread the rhyme each day and try the following ideas as you read:

- Have children clap the syllables.

- Put dots under each word to help children track the words.

- Invite children to find words that rhyme with the last word in each line.

- Have children listen for words that start with the same letter or sound as one of the words.

Roll a Rhyme

Make a paper cube from the pattern on the following page. Write the title of a different rhyme on each side as well as a picture clue. For example, for "Mary Had a Little Lamb," write the title and draw a picture of a little girl with a lamb. A child rolls the cube and then leads the class in saying the rhyme that he rolls.

Vocabulary

Expand the children's vocabulary by asking them to guess what some of the unusual words in rhymes might mean, such as *tuffet, curds,* and *contrary*. Model how to look words up in a dictionary to find definitions.

Nursery Rhyme Club

Make a poster entitled "Nursery Rhyme Club." Whenever a child can say a rhyme, he signs his name on the poster. (If the child cannot sign his name, sign it for him.) Make sure not to exclude children who have a harder time reciting rhymes. Help them to complete it or let them sign for showing effort. It would also be fun to give children a membership card!

Rhyme Puzzles

Write lines of nursery rhymes on sentence strips. Place them in a pocket chart and model reading the rhymes. Mix up the strips and see if children can put them back in order. Because most children cannot yet read at this age, read the sentences aloud or add pictures to the sentence strips to help them.

Dramatize Nursery Rhymes

Encourage the children to act out nursery rhymes. Try some of the following ideas:

- Invite them to play Follow the Leader after dramatizing "Mary Had a Little Lamb."

- Hide paper mittens around the room for children to find ("The Three Little Kittens").

- Turn a block into a candlestick and have the children jump over it for "Jack Be Nimble."

- Provide playdough for children to wrap around their thumbs like a plum for "Little Jack Horner."

Snacks

Tie in cooking activities and snacks with nursery rhymes. For example:

- Eat hard-boiled eggs or make egg salad when you read "Humpty Dumpty."

- Make muffins for "The Muffin Man."

- Mix cottage cheese and fruit and serve for Miss Muffet's curds and whey.

- Ask the children to put their thumb in the middle of the dough of a refrigerated biscuit. Put a spoonful of jelly in the hole, bake, and you'll have Jack's Christmas pie!

Art

Relate the following art projects to nursery rhymes.

- "Humpty Dumpty": Cut out oval (egg) shapes from construction paper for each child. Let them decorate their eggs and then tear them into pieces. Encourage the children to glue them back together.

Additional verse for "Humpty Dumpty" (by Jean Feldman)

So the good children got
Some tape and some glue,
And they fiddled and faddled
'Til he looked like new.
Then they carefully placed him
Back on the wall,
And said, "Humpty Dumpty,
Please don't fall!"

- "Jack and Jill": Help children make finger puppets and act out the rhyme. To make finger puppets, cut out patterns of Jack and Jill from heavy paper. Children color them and cut them out. Make sure to include tabs to make finger puppets. Have the children put them on index fingers as you say the rhyme.

Finger tab

Jack and Jill
Jack and Jill went up the hill
To fetch a pail of water.
Jack fell down and broke his crown,
And Jill came tumbling after.

Additional verses by Jean Feldman:

Then up got Jack and said to Jill
As in his arms he took her.
"You're not hurt. Brush off that dirt.
Now, let's go fetch that water."

So Jack and Jill went up the hill
To fetch a pail of water.
They brought it back to mother dear,
Who thanked her son and daughter.

- "Hickory Dickory Dock": Make paper plate clocks. Help the children draw a clock face on a paper plate and insert a brad in the middle for the clock hands.

Games
Adapt nursery rhyme concepts to games children enjoy playing.

- Substitute a plastic spider for a letter to play a game similar to "A-Tisket, A-Tasket" when reading "Little Miss Muffet."

- Put the children into pairs and have them play a clapping game with "Pat-a-Cake."

- Let each child take off a shoe and hide it around the room for "Diddle Diddle Dumpling."

- Increase the height of a jump rope as children try to jump over it ("Jack Be Nimble").

- Play nursery rhyme charades. Encourage the children to act out different rhymes for their friends to guess.

Hint! Check out these websites for additional activities with nursery rhymes:

curry.edschool.virginia .edu/go/wil/rimes_and _rhymes
mrsdiminnie.com

readwritethink.org

rhymes.org.uk

enchantedlearning.com

Jack be nimble!
Jack be quick!
Jack jumped over
the candlestick!

Nursery Rhyme Notebook

Each child should have a three-ring binder or pocket folder to decorate and use as a nursery rhyme notebook or folder. Each week choose a new poem, song, or rhyme that relates to a classroom theme or something children are interested in. Write the rhyme on a large poster or pocket chart and make individual copies of the rhyme for each child. Increase the font size and double space between the words to accommodate the children's visual needs. The following are some ways to use the rhyme during the week:

- **Monday**: Introduce the poem as a shared reading experience. Reread the poem several times. Let children use pointers to find letters or words they recognize. Point out words that rhyme. "Is there anything that you notice about these words?"

- **Tuesday**: Give children individual copies of the poem. Let them illustrate the poem, hole punch it, and put it in their notebooks.

- **Wednesday**: Use the poem for skill work during small group time. Have children (helping them as needed) find and highlight words that rhyme or begin with the same letter.

- **Thursday**: Ask the children to bring their notebooks to the large group. Reread the week's rhyme and review previous rhymes.

- **Friday**: Invite the children to "read" the rhymes independently or with a buddy. Since most of the children will not be able to read the words, they can recite the poem from memory and look at the words on the page.

- **End your Fridays with "Poetry Café."** Children sit on the floor with their notebooks and take turns reciting their favorite rhymes. Children will get a kick out of snapping their fingers instead of clapping. (This is what the Beat poets did at their poetry readings!)

- **Weekend**: On Friday, have the children take home their nursery rhyme notebooks. Ask them to read or sing the rhyme to someone in their family over the weekend. Ask family members to sign their names and write comments and compliments on each poem.

Fluency Fun!

Use nursery rhymes to enhance children's oral fluency with some of the following strategies:

- **Choral Reading**: Read together as if singing.

- **Shadow Reading**: Read a line and the children repeat.

- **Missing Word**: Omit a word and have the children fill it in.

- **Say What?**: Read the text the wrong way and let the children correct you.

- **Three Bears**: Read like Papa Bear (deep voice), Mama Bear (high-pitched voice), and Baby Bear.

- **Emotions**: Read the nursery rhyme in a happy, sad, mad, scared, or other emotional voice.

- **"Martian" Style**: Place your index fingers up on each side of your head (like antennae) and "beep" for each syllable. Instead of clapping on each syllable, children say "Beep!" throughout the rhyme. The space age meets traditional nursery rhymes! Children will love it!

- **Rainbow**: Open palms and place them on the left side of your body. Curve your arms up and over in an arch as you read each line. Sweep back to the left and read the next line. Have the children do the same.

- **Pirate**: Say, "Arrrgh" and talk out of the side of your mouth like a pirate!

- **Rock-and-Roll**: Try reading the rhymes "rock and roll style," fast, slow, loud, soft, and in any other silly versions the children suggest!

CHAPTER 3

Letters, Letters Everywhere!

Alphabet knowledge, which is the ability to identify and name letters, is a strong predictor of future reading achievement. Post alphabet letters in your classroom; provide a variety of alphabet books; and have an abundance of blocks, magnetic letters, and other materials with letters on them to spark children's interest in these symbols. Always remember that it is more important for children to play with letters, rather than use workbooks or flash cards.

In this chapter, you will find a number of ideas for using alphabet letters in a variety of ways, which will expose children to the alphabet in a natural way.

Classroom Alphabet

Use your classroom walls, bulletin board, file folders, poster board, and so on to expose your children to the alphabet. Anything is possible!

Skill Development

Children will:

- develop alphabet knowledge
- increase print knowledge

Name Alphabet

Use children's names to create a classroom alphabet.
Cut out 26 squares (9" x 9") of cardboard. Write the letters of the alphabet on the cards, one letter per square. Next, glue photos of the children in the class whose names begin with each letter on the squares. For example, glue a picture of a girl named Caroline on the C square. Use first names, last names, or both. Help the children print their names underneath their photos. Glue or draw pictures of common objects on the letter squares without names (for example, glue a picture of a xylophone for X).

Environmental Print

Give each child a letter and ask him to bring in a food label or other piece of environmental print that begins with that sound. For example, if a child had the letter "S" she could bring in the label from a can of soup or a box of spaghetti. Write each letter (uppercase and lowercase) at the top of an 8" x 10" poster board and let children glue their labels underneath the letters. Children could bring in real objects that are lightweight (such as a feather or a leaf) to glue to letter cards.

Family Alphabet

Invite each family to help their child make a poster for one letter of the alphabet. Encourage them to represent the letter any way they want, such as make a collage of objects, draw pictures that begin with the sound, or any other idea. This is a great way to involve families in their child's learning.

Letter Wall

Choose a large, blank wall or bulletin board in your classroom for this project. Write each letter of the alphabet on 4" x 6" rectangles. Attach them to the wall, providing plenty of space around each letter. Increase children's interest in the letters by pointing to the letters as you sing songs, do chants, and play games. Ask each child to bring in the label from her favorite food (breakfast cereal, cookies, snacks, or other food). Help the children cut out the product name on their label. Can they "read" the word? What letter does their word begin with? Can they match their word to the appropriate letter on the wall? Tape their words under the appropriate letters. Read over the words, moving your finger from left to right under the words. Play games such as "I Spy" using the words. Encourage the children to continue bringing in words they can read to add to the wall.

Hint! Send a note to the families about this project so they can reinforce their child's interest in environmental print at home.

Letter Office

Make a "letter office" by gluing a copy of the alphabet letters on the inside of a file folder. Make one for each child. Let the children decorate the outside of their folder. Use the Letter Office in some of the following ways:

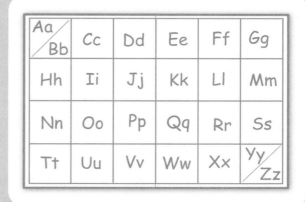

- Have children point to the letters as you sing the following song to the tune of "What Do You Do with a Drunken Sailor."

  This is a tale about the letter A.
  It makes a special sound.
  /a/ /a/ /a/ /a/ A!
  Let's learn another sound.
  This is a tale about the letter B…

- The children use their fingers and point to the letters as they sing the "Alphabet Forward and Backwards," "Who Let the Letters Out?" and other letter songs.

- Use the Letter Office for shared reading. Read the uppercase and lowercase letters, and identify the consonants and vowels. Read in a loud, soft, fast, and slow voice, backwards, and other variations.

- Use this prop to play "I Spy" and other games where children have to identify letters. For example, ask them to find the letter that makes the sound at the beginning of *hop,* find the letters in their names, identify the letter between *G* and *I,* match up magnetic letters with the letters in their offices, and so on.

Hint! Use straws, pencils, or chopsticks for pointers.

Hint! This would be a great project to make at school and send home with activities children can do with their families.

Letters in Centers

Provide more opportunities for children to "play" with letters by adding materials and props with letters as well as writing materials to different learning centers.

Skill Development

Children will:

- increase alphabet knowledge
- develop print connection
- practice invented writing

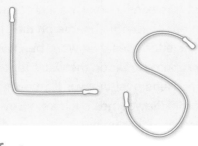

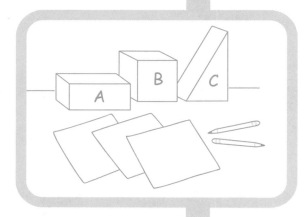

Block Center

Make letter blocks for children to build with. Place unit blocks on tagboard, trace around the blocks to make patterns, and cut them out. Write letters on the tagboard block shapes with markers and tape them to the blocks using clear packaging tape. Encourage the children to build with the letter blocks. Also have paper and pencils available in the center so children can make signs, labels, and illustrations for their creations.

Writing Center

Provide letter stamps and stamp pads, paper, pencils, pens with different colors of ink, markers, envelopes, sticky notes, junk mail, blank books, and a wide variety of paper for the children to play with. Invite them to "write" letters to each other, family members, and other friends.

Manipulatives

Provide letter tiles, Lego letters, letter puzzles, magnetic letters, letter beads, foam letters, and other manipulatives with letters on them for children to explore.

Home Living Center

Place pencils, note pads, grocery lists, magazines, old menus, catalogs, junk mail, and other print material in this center. Encourage the children to use these items in their play (restaurant, grocery store, other kinds of shops, and so on).

Sand and Water Table

Hang a chart of alphabet letters next to the sand table and encourage children to trace their names and letters in the sand. Write letters on ping-pong balls and have children scoop them from the water table with a fish net. See if they can identify the letters they scoop from the water.

Library Center

Provide children with a variety of alphabet books, as well as child-created letter books. Children will also enjoy using felt letters on a flannel board.

Listening Center

Provide tapes of alphabet songs and tapes of alphabet books for children to listen to as they follow along in the book.

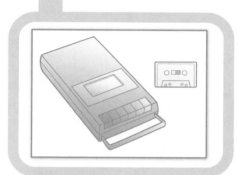

Outdoors

Use chalk to draw giant alphabet letters on the sidewalk or blacktop. Invite children to walk, tiptoe, hop, skip, bounce a ball, and so on around the letter shapes. Give children jump ropes and challenge them to make letters with their ropes. Can their friends identify the letters?

Large Motor

Write letters on beach balls. The children throw the balls to each other and try to identify the letters where their thumbs are when they catch the ball.

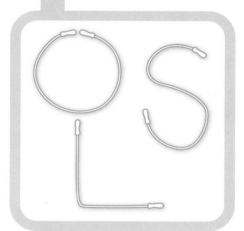

Letter Props

Putting letters on props help children focus on letters in a fun way. The following are some ideas for props you can make and use in your classroom to help the children focus on letters.

Skill Development

Children will:

- develop eye-hand coordination
- track print from left to right
- reinforce concepts about letters and words

Pointers

Using pointers helps children focus their attention on printed letters and helps them track the letters in their letter office, books, or other print materials.

- **Give Me Five:** Cut a small hand shape from cardboard, staple it to a straw, and use it to "tap" letters and words.

- **"Eye" Can!:** Glue a wiggle eye to the end of a jumbo craft stick. Remind children to "keep their eyes" on the letters as you sing "The Alphabet Song."

- **Magic Wand:** Give each child a chopstick. Have them dip one end in glue and then dip it in glitter. The children can use these wands to track letters or words.

- **Witch's Nail:** Purchase these around Halloween at a party supply store. Give one to each child to track letters or words.

- **Pretzel Rod:** Have children track letters or words with a pretzel rod, and then eat it!

- **Bubble Wand:** Bubble wands are fun for framing letters or words.

- **Magnifying Glass:** Help children bend a pipe cleaner to look like a magnifying glass. This is a great tool for children to use to search for letters or words in the classroom.

- **Giant Pointer:** Cover a cardboard roller from a pants hanger with shiny paper or foil and use it for classroom activities.

Letter Wand

Remove the netting from a butterfly net and add some colorful ribbons. (You can find these at most dollar stores.) Another idea is to cut the center out of a plastic flyswatter and use it to frame letters. Sing the following song to the tune of "Do You Know the Muffin Man?"

> *Do you see the letter* (name a letter),
> *The letter ____, the letter ____?*
> *Do you see the letter _____,*
> *Somewhere in the room?*

A child takes the wand, finds the letter, and frames the letter as she sings:

> *Yes, I see the letter ____,*
> *The letter ____, the letter ____.*
> *Yes, I see the letter ____*
> *In the room.*

Giant Keyboard

This giant keyboard is sure to capture the interest of young children. You will need an opaque shower curtain liner, permanent markers, and a clean flyswatter for this project. (If you are uncomfortable using a flyswatter, have children use their hands or other pointers for the activities.) Make an overhead transparency of the keyboard (see illustration). Cut the shower curtain in half and tape it to a wall. Project the transparency on the shower curtain so you can trace around the pattern to make the keyboard. Place the giant keyboard on the floor. Let the children take turns using the flyswatter to point to letters they know. Can they "type" their names? Use the keyboard for matching uppercase and lowercase letters, identifying beginning sounds, typing simple words, and so on.

Hint! Write letters and numerals in different colors.

Letter Beanbags

Play the following games with letter beanbags for fun ways to expose children to letters. You can purchase letter beanbags or make your own. To make your own, cut felt into 5" squares and sew three sides closed. Fill with one half cup of pebbles or small stones and sew the fourth side closed. Cut letters out of felt and glue them to the beanbags.

Hint! Make one side of the beanbag out of red felt and the other side out of blue felt. Glue a lowercase letter cut out of red felt to the blue side, and an uppercase letter cut out of blue felt to the red side.

- **Toss and Catch:** Give the children beanbags to toss and catch. Walk around the room and ask children to identify the letter on their beanbag.

- **Balance:** Identify the letters on the beanbags as you pass them out to children. Ask the children to place the beanbags on their heads and walk around the room. If the beanbags fall off their heads, they stop, put them back on, and start walking again.

- **Song Props:** Use beanbags when singing different alphabet songs. (See pages 64–66 in Chapter 5 for song ideas.) Children toss their beanbags in the air, place them on the floor, or do other movements as their letter is sung.

- **Making Words:** Have children place their beanbags on the floor to form names or simple words.

Letter Badges

Purchase plastic name badge holders at an office supply store. (Or save them from conferences.) Choose one or two different letters each day and write them on paper cut to fit the name badge. Select different children each day to wear the badges. Have children stand up as you sing the following song to the tune of "Jimmy Crack Corn."

Here is a letter, its name is (identify letter).
Here is a letter, its name is ____.
Here is a letter, its name is ____.
And it says (/sound/ /sound/ /sound/).

- Let the child wearing the badge call on her classmates to say words that start with their letters.

- Challenge children to call friends by the letter they are wearing instead of their real names. For example, "D, come sit by me."

- You could also make letter bracelets from empty tape rolls by writing uppercase and lowercase letters all over the rolls.

Letter Blocks

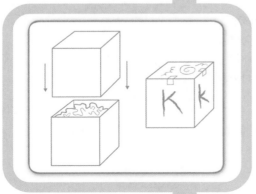

Make letter blocks with the children. You will need two clean (washed and dried) milk cartons for each child, construction paper, newspaper, markers, each child's photo, and clear packaging tape. Stuff one milk carton with newspaper. Insert the second milk carton on top to create a cube. Cut out six pieces of construction paper to fit on the sides of the cube. Help the child write her name on one section, the letter her name begins with in uppercase on one section and lowercase on another section, and glue her photo to another section. The child decorates the remaining two sections with pictures of things she likes. Glue each square to the cube and wrap the block in clear packaging tape.

Children can use these blocks for building in the Block Center, to make comparisons by stacking the blocks like a bar graph in the Math Center, and when singing name songs.

Letter Tubs

Make letter tubs using small plastic containers. Write letters on the tubs, and then fill with small toys or objects that begin with that sound. Introduce one tub at a time. Invite the children to explore the objects and play with them. Have the children name the items. Can they think of other things that could be put in the tub that start with the same sound? Place the tub in a center with paper, pencils, and crayons and encourage the children to write the letter and draw pictures of the objects. As you add new letter tubs, store them on a special shelf in your classroom to encourage children to "revisit" them.

■ ■ ■ ■ ■ ■
Hint! Make additional blocks so all the letters of the alphabet are represented. Demonstrate how to put the blocks together to make words.

■ ■ ■ ■ ■ ■
Hint! This would be a great family project. Give each child a tub with a letter on it and have them fill it with a family member's help.

CHAPTER 4

Names Are Magic!: Making Connections With Children's Names

Young children are naturally egocentric. They love themselves, and they love their names! Use their names to encourage their interest in print, letters, and sounds. Display their names, use them for labels and classroom transitions, insert their names into silly songs, and use them to make rhymes!

Name Games

Children's names are a natural place to begin their letter journey! A young child may see the letter that his name starts with and say, "That's my name!" Use the first letter in a different child's name each day as a springboard for introducing letters with the following activities.

Skill Development

Children will:

- gain alphabet knowledge
- increase print knowledge
- increase self-esteem

Mystery Name

Before doing this activity, make a letter necklace for each child. Cut out 3" circles from poster board, write the first letter of each child's name on one circle, punch a hole in it, and thread it on a piece of 24" string to make a necklace for each child. (Use gold or silver poster board, if desired.) After you decide on the letter of the day, place the necklace in your lap and do a little "drum roll" by tapping your hands on your knees. Give clues about the child's name as you write the letters on the board. For example, "The mystery name today has four letters. You hear the /l/ sound at the end of the name. There is a vowel that sounds like /a/ after the first letter."

- A variation is to play a game similar to Hangman. The children call out letters and you place them on the lines as they appear in the name.

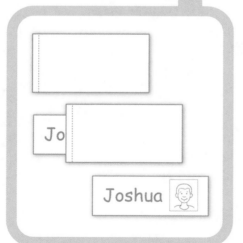

Sneak a Peek

Cut off the left edge of an envelope. Write one child's name on a 12" sentence strip and glue his picture on the right end as shown in the illustration. Place the sentence strip inside the envelope and carefully pull out the sentence strip to reveal one letter at a time. Invite the children to blend the sounds of the letters and predict whose name will appear.

Cheer the Name

Cheer the child's name. For example, "Give me a W!" "W!" "Give me an I!" "I!"

Name Songs

- Sing the following song to the tune "The Bear Went over the Mountain," substituting the first letter of the child's name.

  W is for Will,
  W is for Will,
  W is for Will,
  And he's a friend of mine.

- You can also sing the letters in their names to the tune of "Bingo." For example:

  There is a friend that we all know,
  And Will is his name-o.
  _W-i-l-l, W-i-l-l, W-i-l-l,_
  That's how you spell his name-o.

- Sing the "Birthday Song" and substitute the first letter of each word with the first letter of the child's name. For example, if the child's name is Will, sing, "Wappy wirthday wo wou..." If a child's name starts with a vowel, then use the first letter in his last name.

- Use the child's name and first letter in his name in "Pat-a-Cake."

  Pat-a-cake, pat-a-cake, baker's man.
  Bake me a cake as fast as you can.
  Roll it, and pat it, and mark it with W.
  And throw it in the oven for Will and me!

Sign Language

Using the American Manual Alphabet, learn the sign for the first letter in each child's name.

Name Puzzle

Write each child's name on a 10" sentence strip. Cut between the letters in the name and put them in an envelope. Write the child's name on the front of the envelope. The children empty the envelopes and put the letters together like a puzzle to spell their names.

Syllables

Invite the children to clap, snap, wiggle their hips, or make other motions for the syllables in a child's name. Use the child's first and last name, if desired, to make this more challenging.

Rhyme Game

Have the children think of words that rhyme with their special friend's name. (They don't have to be "real" words, as long as they rhyme.)

Sounds Like...

Make a list on chart paper of other words that begin with the same letter as the child's name. Write the words as the children call them out. Say the letters out loud as you print them on the chart. Read over the chart together, sweeping your hand from left to right under each word.

■ To extend the activity, call out words and ask the children to give a "thumbs up" if the word begins like the first letter of the child's name or a "thumbs down" if the word does not begin with the letter.

Giant Letters

Write the first letter in the child's name on a large piece of poster board and cut it out. Send the large cutout letter home with the child with instructions for family members to help him make a collage on it with pictures, photos, environmental print, and so on.

Name Bottle

Hint! Add water and glitter to the bottle and seal tightly closed, if desired.

Place letter beads that spell the child's first name in an empty, plastic water bottle. Tape the child's picture and name to the outside of the bottle. Challenge children to find the letters in the bottle and spell the name.

Flap Book

Turn a brown paper lunch bag horizontally and keep it folded closed. Fold over the end of brown paper lunch bags as shown in the illustration. Open the flap and print the child's name so that only the first letter will show when you fold over the flap. Glue the child's picture under the flap.

Name Cards

Children can learn a lot by using something as simple as name cards. Write each child's name on an 8" sentence strip and place the cards in a box or basket. Use the name cards in activities similar to those below to enhance name recognition, reading skills, writing skills, and classroom management.

Skill Development

Children will:

- gain alphabet knowledge
- increase print knowledge
- develop visual memory
- learn name recognition

Name Strips

To start, put children's photos next their names on the sentence strips. After several weeks, when children are more confident and can recognize their names, make another set of cards. Let each child choose a symbol (sticker, animal, shape, and so on) to put beside his name in place of his photo. When children have mastered reading the names and symbols, make another set of cards and write the first letter of the names in a different color. Finally, write each child's name on a sentence strip using one color of ink, no symbols, and no photos.

Songs

Cover a small box with red construction paper and put the name cards in the box. Choose one card a time as you sing the following songs:

(Tune: "Polly Wolly Doodle")
I wish I had a little red box
To put my (name on the card) *in.* (for example, …to put my Kyle in)
I'd take him (or her) *out and go,*
"How do you do!" (pretend to shake a hand)
And put him back again!

(Tune: "Skip to My Lou")
Hello, (name), *how are you?*
Hello, (name), *how are you?*
Hello, (name), *how are you?*
We're so glad to see you.

Hickety pickety bumblebee,
Who can say this name for me?
(say a child's name)
Clap it. (clap the syllables as you say the name)
Snap it. (snap the syllables as you say the name)
Whisper it. (whisper the name)

Transitions

Select name cards to call on children to line up, answer questions, go to centers, and so on.

Helpers

Choose name cards from the box to assign helpers for the day, special jobs, to sit next to you, and so on. (**Note:** Make sure everyone has equal turns!)

Writing Center

Keep a set of name cards in the Writing Center so children can use their friends' names to write stories or notes.

Word Wall

Attach Velcro or tape to the back of the name cards and use them for interactive activities on your classroom word wall.

Seating

Place cards on the rug before Circle or Group Time. Have children find their name and sit in that spot.

Hint! You can also punch holes in the cards and keep them on a ring.

Grouping

Pull out two names at a time to choose pairs for partner activities. Pull out four name cards for small group activities.

Smart Cookies

This is an alternative to Name Cards. Instead of cards, children use "name cookies" for activities. Cut out cookie shapes (circular or gingerbread shape) from poster board or fun foam. Write each child's name on a cookie. Have the children decorate their cookies with crayons or markers and then glue the children's photos to the cookies, if desired. Attach a piece of magnetic tape to the back of each cookie.

Use the cookies for:

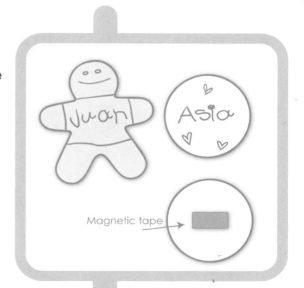

- **Sign in:** Children find their cookies and place them on the board when they arrive each day.

- **Songs:** Have them hold up the appropriate "cookies" as you sing name songs.

- **Sorting:** Use them to sort names by beginning sounds, syllables, and so on.

- **Comparisons:** Write three or four different pizza toppings on the board. Children place their name under the topping they like best. Help them count the number of cookies under each response. Which had the most? Least? Use cookies for other comparisons, such as favorite pets, songs, book titles, colors, and so on.

Classroom Photos

Take photographs of the children in your room. Trim the photos to 2 ½" squares and glue them on several sheets of paper. Make multiple copies to use in the following projects.

Hint! Reduce photos to 1" and glue them around the edges of a sheet of copy paper to make a border. Run off multiple copies and use it for notes to parents or for additional paper in the Writing Center.

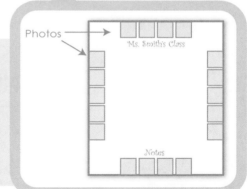

Lotto Match

Cut out one set of photos and glue them to a piece of cardboard with a 3" grid. Have the children take a second set of photos and match them with the same pictures.

Concentration

You will need two copies of each photo. Cut out 3" squares from poster board and glue photos to the squares. Place the squares face down on the table and use them to play a memory game. Have children try to match pictures by turning over two at a time and remembering where they are.

Pocket Chart

Write children's names on sentence strips and place the sentence strips and photos in a pocket chart. Have the children try to match the names with the pictures.

People Puppets

Cut out full body photos and glue them to jumbo craft sticks. Children can use the puppets for oral language activities.

Graphing

Use photos for graphs and comparisons.

Art Projects

Let children cut out outlines or photos of their faces and use them for various art projects. For example, they could draw a picture of what they want to be when they grow up around their face, draw themselves as their favorite storybook character, make a collage with their friends' pictures, and so on.

Classroom Books

Photographs or self-portraits are great to use for classroom books.

N is for Natalie.
/n/ /n/ /n/
Natalie starts with N.
/n/ /n/ /n/

That's My Sound!

This book is a natural way to expose children to letters and sounds. First, you will need a photograph (or self-portrait) for each child. Glue each child's photo on a piece of paper. Write the uppercase and lowercase letter that the child's name begins with on either side of his picture. Glue a copy of the words to the song below to the bottom of the page. Sing and read to the tune of "Where Is Thumbkin?"

Teacher: *N is for Natalie.*
Children: *N is for Natalie.*
Teacher: */n/ /n/ /n/*
Children: */n/ /n/ /n/*
Teacher: *Natalie starts with N.*
Children: *Natalie starts with N.*
Teacher: */n/ /n/ /n/*
Children: */n/ /n/ /n/*

Start your day by reading and singing the song. Invite the children to name other words that begin with the same sound.

Hello Book

This book is perfect for helping children recognize their names and create friendships. You will need a photograph of each child, construction paper, book rings, and markers. Glue each child's photo on a page. Write "Hello, (child's name)." at the top of the page. Punch holes in the pages and put them together with book rings. Use the book in the following ways:

- **Circle or Group Time**: Start your day by reading the book together and saying hello to each other.

- **Questions**: Use the book when you want to ask the class questions. Randomly turn to a page and call on that child to answer the question. This will allow "thinking time" and discourage children from shouting out the answer.

- **Transitions**: Use this book to dismiss children for learning centers, to line up, and other transitions. Flip through the book and hold up different pictures. As the children see their photo, they may be dismissed, line up, and so on.

- **Songs**: Sing and read this book to the tune of "Good Night, Ladies."

   Hello, (child's name).
   Hello, (child's name).
   Hello, (child's name).
   How are you today?

Mystery Classmate Game

This is a great game to play every day. It involves all of the children and is a fun way to introduce writing conventions to them.

Skill Development:

Children will:

- develop print knowledge
- increase self-esteem
- practice tracking from left to right

Each day, choose a different child to write about for this special activity. Write "Mystery Classmate" at the top of a piece of paper. Explain to the children that they are "detectives" and have to figure out who the classmate is from the clues (for clues, use physical attributes, child's likes, and special talents).

For example, say, "Clue number one: My eyes are brown." (Say each letter out loud as you write it.) Encourage the children to read over the clue as you track the words from left to right. Say, "Hmmm? Who could this be?" Give the children a minute to guess, then say, "Clue number two: I like to draw flowers and bees." Continue writing clues as the children try to guess who the child is. Call attention to different writing conventions. "An uppercase letter tells me where to start. I better not forget the period at the end. It tells me when to stop."

Read over all the clues and end by writing "Who am I?" The children will be proud of their detective work as they disclose the mystery person, and the mystery child gets to decorate the paper by gluing on his photo, drawing a self-portrait, illustrating his likes and talents, and so on. Roll up the poster at the end of the day so the child can take it home and hang it in his house.

CHAPTER 5

La-La-La-La Letters!: Sing to Learn Letters And Sounds

Music is the most convenient way to learn anything! Singing alphabet songs can provide children with early knowledge about letter names and sounds. Think of these songs as a filing system in the brain. As children repeat letters and sounds in a musical way, they are reinforcing concepts in a playful and magical way.

Singing Sounds

Singing songs that focus on letters and their sounds helps children learn the alphabet in a fun, meaningful way.

Skill Development:

Children will:
- increase alphabet knowledge
- practice oral language
- improve auditory memory
- develop phonological awareness

Traditional ABC Forward and Backwards

Sing the traditional "Alphabet Song" slowly as you point to the letters on your classroom alphabet chart. Challenge the children to sing it backwards. End the backwards version by singing, "Now I've said my Z Y Xs. Bet that's not what you expected!"

Alphabet Sounds

Sing the traditional alphabet song, but instead of saying the letters, make the letter sounds (/a/ /b/ /c/ /d/ /e/ /f/ /g/, and so on).

100 Bottles of Pop

Sing letters to the tune of "100 Bottles of Pop on the Wall." Alternate crossing and tapping right hand to left knee and left hand to right knee to the beat.

A B C D E F G
H I J K L M
N O P Q
R S T U
V W X Y Z

There are many familiar tunes you can use to sing the alphabet, such as "I've Been Working on the Railroad," "Amazing Grace," and the "Gilligan's Island" theme song. This is a fun way to sing the alphabet with the children!

If Your Name Begins with...

Use this song to develop listening skills and letter recognition. Make up verses similar to the ones below to the tune of "If You're Happy and You Know It."

If your name begins with A, clap your hands…
If your name begins with B, stomp your feet…
If your name begins with C, nod your head…
If your name begins with D, wiggle around…

Alphabet Farm

Sing "Old MacDonald Had a Farm" and replace animal names with letters. For example:

(Your name) had an alphabet,
She loved letters so.
And in her alphabet there was an H.
And it would always go,
/h/ /h/ here,
And a /h/ /h/ there.
Here a /h/, there a /h/.
Everywhere a /h/ /h/.
(Your name) had an H.
She loved letters so.

Continue using other letters and sounds in the song.

Letters Go 'Round

Place a large cutout letter on the floor. The children hold hands and circle around the letter as they sing the following song to the tune of "Here We Go 'Round the Mulberry Bush." Insert different letters each time you sing the song. For example:

Here we go 'round the letter k,
The letter k, the letter k,
Here we go 'round the letter k
So early in the morning.
/k/ /k/ /k/ is what it will say,
What it will say, what it will say.
/k/ /k/ /k/ is what it will say.
It's the letter k.

Continue placing other letters on the floor and singing the song.

In My Mouth

Sing this song to the tune of "He's Got the Whole World in His Hands." Make the manual signs for the letters as you sing.

> *I've got the whole alphabet in my mouth.*
> *I've got the whole alphabet in my mouth.*
> *I've got the whole alphabet in my mouth,*
> *And I can read!*
>
> *I've got "A" /a/ /a/ in my mouth.*
> *I've got "B" /b/ /b/ in my mouth.*
> *I've got "C" /c/ /c/ in my mouth,*
> *And I can read!*

Continue singing about each letter as you make its sound. End with, "I've got all the letters in my mouth and I'm ready to read!"

Give children a small mirror to look at their mouth and tongue as they make different sounds.

In My Mouth Book

Make a class book to go along with this song. Take a close-up photo of each child with her mouth open wide. Cut out small alphabet letters from construction paper and glue them to the children's photos as shown in the illustration. Write the appropriate verse on each page. For example, on the page for the child who has the letter D in her mouth, write: *I've got "D" /d/ /d/ in my mouth.* Put the pages together in alphabetical order and bind with book rings.

Deck the Room

Sing the following song to the tune of "Deck the Halls."

> *Deck the room with letters and sounds. A B C D E F G*
> *Listen up and look around. H I J K L M N O P*
> *Get a book and you will see Q R S T U V*
> *Words and letters read with me W X Y and Z.*

After singing the song, talk about all the letters and sounds in your classroom. Take the children on a "word hunt." Can the children find a word for each letter? For example, A is for alphabet (/a/ /a/ /a/), B is for boys (/b/ /b/ /b/), C is for cafeteria (/c/ /c/ /c/), and so on. Change the words to match the environmental print in your classroom.

Using Props

Using props such as flashlights and letter bears add an extra dimension to the songs. After all, flashlights are fun and bears are cute!

Skill Development

Children will:

- increase alphabet knowledge
- gain an interest in print

Shine On!

You will need a flashlight for this activity. Turn off the lights in the room and sing the song below to the tune of "Shine On, Harvest Moon" inserting different letters.

Shine on, shine on the letter ___,
And make it glow.
Shine on, shine on letter ____,
It's a letter that we know.

Pass the flashlight to a child and ask her to shine the light on the letter wherever she sees it in the classroom (chalkboard messages, alphabet chart, environmental print, bulletin board displays, word wall, and so on). Continue singing other letters for the children to identify. You could also let the children take turns singing words instead of letters in the song.

- Another tune you can use with a flashlight is "This Little Light of Mine."

    This little light of mine, I'm going to let it shine.
    This little light of mine, I'm going to let it shine.
    This little light of mine, I'm going to let it shine.
    Shine on, (letter),
    Shine on, (letter),
    Shine on, (letter).

Hint! The flashlight is also a useful tool for tracking a line of print as you read.

Letter Bears

Letter bears are a fun way for children to look at letters and learn letter recognition. Cut out 26 bears from construction paper. Write a different letter (uppercase and lowercase) on each bear.

- Sing the following song to the tune of "Twinkle, Twinkle, Little Star" as you hold up the bears.

  (First letter) *bear,* (first letter) *bear, what do you see?*
  I see (second letter) *bear looking at me.*
  (Second letter) *bear,* (second letter) *bear, what do you see?*
  I see (third letter) *bear looking at me….*

- Transitions: Use the bears to dismiss children for centers or to line up by having them look for the bear with the letter at the beginning of their name.

- Use letter bears to assess children's recognition of letters.

Letter Signs

Letter signs create interest and focus children's attention in a wide variety of activities. You will need 26 plastic sheet protectors, paper, and string to make these. Make large copies of each letter on 8 ½" x 11" sheets of paper and place each letter in a sheet protector. Punch two holes in the top of each and thread a piece of string through so children can slip it over their heads easily.

Choose five children to wear the letter sign. Explain the difference between letter names and letter sounds. "All letters have names (such as A, B, and C), and they each make a different sound (/a/, /b/, and /c/). Letters come in two sizes: uppercase (or capital) letters and lowercase letters. But they both make the same sound!" Name the letters the children are wearing and make the letter sounds. Have the five children hold hands and skip around in a circle as you sing the song below to the tune of "Five Little Ducks." As you make a sound in the song, the child wearing that letter skips back to you.

Five little letters went out one day (hold up five fingers)
Over the hills and far away. (move hand up and down)
When the teacher called /m/, /m/, /m/, /m/, (make sound)
Only the letter "M" came back.

Continue singing about the other letters.

- Sing the traditional "Alphabet Song" as children wear the sign. Have each child stand when her letter is sung.

> **Hint!** Write the lowercase letter on one side of the sign and the uppercase letter on the other side. Place a star next to the lowercase letter to help children identify it.

> **Hint!** Make the consonants on blue paper and the vowels on red paper.

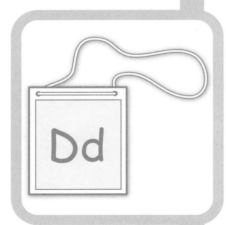

- Play a guessing game by singing the following song to the tune of "Go In and Out the Window."

  I'm looking for the letter.
  I'm looking for the letter.
  I'm looking for the letter.
  That always goes /m/.

  The child wearing M stands up as the class sings:

  M is the letter.
  M is the letter.
  M is the letter.
  That always goes /m/.

- Invite several children to come to the front of the room and hold hands to make words.

Letter Exercising

It's time for the children to exercise their bodies and brains with these fun, letter-oriented movement activities!

Skill Development

Children will:

- develop alphabet knowledge
- practice motor skills
- gain phonological awareness

Lettercise

Put your hands in the air and say a letter, touch your waist and make the letter sound, and then touch the ground and say a word that begins with that sound. For example:

A (hands in the air), /a/ (hands on waist), *ant* (touch the ground)

B (hands in the air), /b/ (hands on waist), *bear* (touch the ground)

Letter Punch

Call out letters, and punch your hand over the opposite side of your body as you make the letter sound. For example, call out "A," then say the letter sound (/a/) as you punch your right hand to the left. Call out "B," and say the letter sound (/b/) as you punch your left hand to the right.

March, Jump, Dance

Do a variety of movements as you sing the traditional "Alphabet Song." March, jump, tiptoe, or make other movements as you say letters. Demonstrate how to do the "disco" by putting one hand on your hip and the index finger from the other hand in the air. Move your hand from the top to the bottom across your body as you sing letters.

Yo Letters!

Get your elbows up, get loose, and get ready to do this chant like a rapper!

> *Yo, A,* (move arms and dance around)
> *What do you say?*
> *When we make your sound*
> *It will go this way*
> */a/ /a/ /a/ /a/ /a/ /a/ /a/ /a/ /a/* (bring fists together and make a circular
>   motion)

> *Yo, B,*
> *What do you say?*
> *When we make your sound*
> *It will go this way*
> */b/ /b/ /b/ /b/ /b/ /b/ /b/ /b/ /b/*

Continue with the rest of the alphabet.

■ Assign each child a letter of the alphabet. It might be the first letter in their first name, the first letter of their last name, or any random letter. Sit in a circle on the floor. As you chant the child's letter, she gets in the middle of the circle and does a silly dance.

"BINGO" Letter Cards

Cut poster board into five 8" x 10" sections. Write the letters "B," "I," "N," "G," and "O" on the front of the cards. On the back of the cards, write the

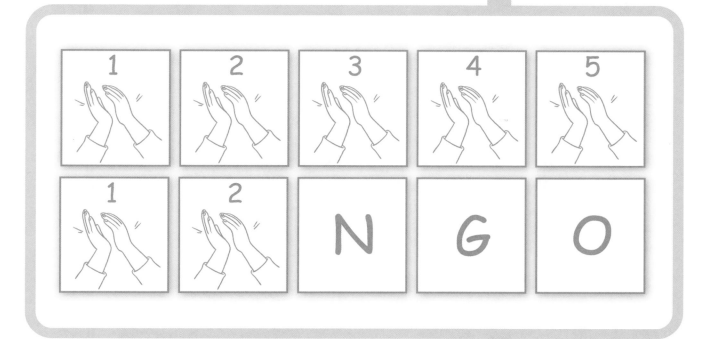

numerals 1–5. Draw hands that look like they are clapping below the numerals.

Choose five children to come to the front of the room to hold the letter cards. Say each letter on the card as you point to it. Count the letters. Explain, "Each of our friends is holding a letter. But when we put those letters together, we make a word. These letters spell the name of a dog we like to sing about. Does anybody know what B-I-N-G-O spells?" Sing the first verse of the song. Stop and have the child holding the "B" turn over her letter. "I see the numeral 1 and hands clapping. That means this time instead of singing B, we will clap." Continue until all the letters are turned over and you are clapping the song.

Introduce other letters by changing the words of the song. For example, "There was a bear all furry and brown and Fuzzy was his name-o. F-U-Z-Z-Y…" Or, "There is a color we all like and green is it's name-o. G-R-E-E-N…" Emphasize how we put letters together to make words.

Feel! Taste! Touch!: Multi-Sensory Materials To Activate Senses and Engage Children in Hands-on Learning

How does information get to the brain? Children need to see, hear, feel, taste, and touch to learn new information. Sitting in front of a computer only activates a small portion of the brain. That's why hands-on materials that stimulate many areas of the brain are essential in a young child's world.

Feel, Taste, and Touch!

Senses are like pathways to the brain. The more senses you activate, the more likely the message is going to get there. And through repetition, the message is going to stay there!

Skill Development

Children will:

- increase alphabet knowledge
- improve small motor skills
- develop print connection

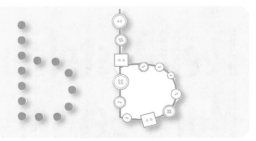

Photo Sheet

Make dot-to-dot letters on a sheet of paper. Make as many copies as needed. Have the children connect the dots with a marker or other materials. Children can also outline the letters with counting bears, shells, buttons, and other manipulatives.

Rainbow Writing

Children make "rainbow letters" by tracing around letters with different colors of crayons.

■ ■ ■ ■ ■ ■
Hint! Make giant rainbow letters using bulletin board paper on the wall.

Scratch-and-Sniff

Help children write letters with glue. Sprinkle the letters with powdered gelatin or powdered drink mix. Let it dry, and then scratch and sniff!

Lotty Dotty

Use a marker to make dotted letters. Put a drop of glue on top of each dot. Let dry. Have the children trace over the dots of dried glue with their finger as they make the letter sound.

■ ■ ■ ■ ■ ■
Hint! Place a small piece of sponge in a spring-type clothespin and use as a paintbrush.

Magic Paintbrush

Give children a clean paintbrush and a cup of water. Have them make letters on a chalkboard and then watch them disappear!

Mystery Letter

Write letters with a white crayon. Children dip a large paintbrush into diluted paint and "wash" over the entire page to make the letter appear.

Pretzel ABCs

Give children pretzel sticks and pretzel twists for snack. Have them nibble the pretzels to make letters.

Squirt and Eat

Provide squirt cheese to make letters on crackers. Children lick the letters with their tongue. You can also try this with squeeze icing on sugar cookies.

Letter Bread

Make letter bread with the children. Mix ¼ cup milk with a few drops of food coloring. Children use Q-tips to make letters on the bread with the colored milk. Toast. Serve with butter or honey.

Hint! You can also thaw frozen bread dough and let the children form it into letters. Bake and eat.

Alphabet Cereal, Crackers, and Pretzels

Serve letter-shaped snack foods for snack and challenge children to identify letters, make words, and then eat.

Letter Transfer

Children move foam letters from one plate to another plate with tongs. A variation is for children to move plastic letters from one bowl to another with a spoon.

Letter Bottles

Invite families to help their children make Letter Bottles using plastic water bottles. Give each child a plastic bottle to take home that has the first letter of their name written on it. Challenge them to find objects around their house that begin with their letter and will fit inside the bottle.

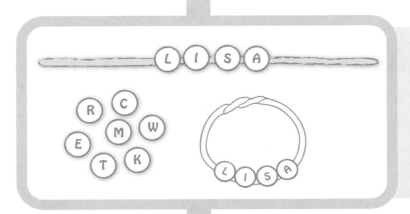

Letter Beads

Children string plastic beads with letters on them on a pipe cleaner to make a bracelet. Help them spell out their names or other special words.

■ ■ ■ ■ ■ ■
Hint! Make your own letter beads. Purchase large wooden beads at a craft store and write letters on them with a permanent marker. Children string them on a shoelace.

■ ■ ■ ■ ■ ■
Hint! To give the playdough a nice scent, substitute baby oil or aromatherapy oil for the vegetable oil. You can also add unsweetened Kool-aid powder, vanilla, cinnamon, or other spices to give it an aroma.

Playdough Letters

Write letters on clear plastic plates, plastic placemats, sheet protectors, or leftover laminating film with a permanent marker. Make playdough using the recipe below. Children roll the playdough into snakes and place it on top of the letters. Can they make objects that begin with that sound?

Homemade Playdough
2 cups flour
2 tbsp. cream of tartar
2 tbsp. vegetable oil
2 cups water
food coloring

Mix ingredients together in a pan until smooth. Cook over medium heat, stirring constantly until the mixture forms a ball and sticks to the spoon. Cool and knead. Store in resealable bag.

Snip, Sew, Trace Letters

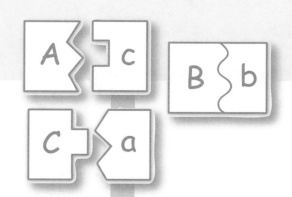

Stencils

Have children trace around letter stencils on construction paper. Children can cut out the letters after tracing around them. If desired, children can make letter necklaces by punching holes in the letters and stringing them on yarn.

Sewing Cards

Write letters on paper plates. Punch holes around the edges and have children sew with a shoelace. You can also use plastic placemats to make large letters.

Letter Puzzles

Write uppercase and lowercase letters on 8" x 6" pieces of poster board. Cut puzzle designs between the letters. Children will know if they've matched uppercase and lowercase letters correctly because they will fit together perfectly.

Letter Collage

Give children old magazines, catalogs, and newspapers. Have them cut out letters and glue them on a sheet of construction paper. Can they name the letters that they cut out? Challenge them to cut out all the letters in their names. Can they find all the letters from A–Z?

Sign Language Letters

Skill Development

Children will:

- increase alphabet knowledge
- develop small motor skills
- understand print connection

Sing and Sign

Teach the children ASL signs for letters as they are introduced. Sing the following song to the tune of "Where Is Thumbkin?" to reinforce the concept.

> Teacher: *Where is A?*
> Children: *Where is A?* (children repeat)
> Teacher: *Here I am!* (hold up a sign of the manual sign for A)
> Children: *Here I am!* (children repeat and copy sign)
> Teacher: *What do you say A?*
> Children: *What do you say A?*
> Teacher: */a/ /a/ /a/*
> Children: */a/ /a/ /a/*

Make visuals similar to the one shown by enlarging the signs on the following page. Pass these out for the children to hold up at the appropriate place in the song.

Letter Box

Sing the following song to the tune of "Polly Wolly Doodle" to teach children manual signs for letters.

> *I wish I had a letter box*
> *To put my A in.* (hold up sign for manual A)
> *I'd take it out and say,*
> *"/a/ /a/ /a/"*
> *And put it back again.* (pretend to put hand back in box)

Continue singing about other letters and making signs as you sing.

Sign and Spell

Use sign language to spell children's names and other words. Encourage children to spell their own names using sign language.

Transitions

Tell the children to watch your hand. As you make the sign that the child's name begins with, he may line up, go to centers, wash his hands, and so on.

Signing Game

Make different signs and see if the children can guess the letter you are making. What sound does that letter make? What is a word that begins with that sound?

A to Z Signs

Sing the "Alphabet Song" as you sign each letter.

■ ■ ■ ■ ■ ■
Hint! Encourage the children to make "strong" letters. As children tighten muscles in their hands, they will also strengthen those small motor skills.

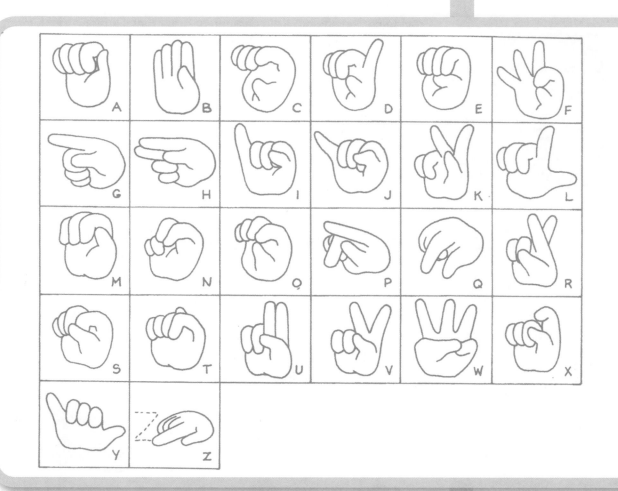

Marvelous Magnetic Letters

Use magnetic letters for the following activities to give children hands-on experiences to discover letters.

Skill Development

Children will:

- increase alphabet knowledge
- practice visual matching
- develop concept of words

Letter Sticks

Glue magnetic letters to jumbo craft sticks. Have the children use these to match letters on print found in the classroom. They can also find objects in the room beginning with the sound the letter makes.

Letter Play

Provide cookie sheets, a file cabinet, or other metal surface for children to place magnetic letters on. Encourage them to make words with the letters.

■ ■ ■ ■ ■ ■

Hint! Store letters in an empty cookie tin, and let children make words on the lid.

Sand Box Treasure

Hide magnetic letters in the sand table. Children use a magnet to find letters. Have them identify the letters they "attract."

Letter Password

Place several letters the children are learning around the metal door frame of your classroom door. As children leave the room, ask them to touch a particular letter. (You could also ask them to touch the letter they hear at the beginning of a particular word.)

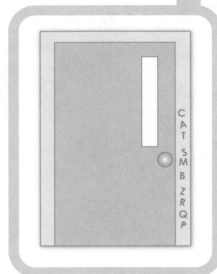

Letter Match-Up

Create a class alphabet book by asking children to draw pictures for each letter. Place an outline of the magnetic letter at the top of the appropriate pages. Have the children match the magnetic letters with the outlines in the book.

Letter Hunt

Hide letters around the classroom. Children will love to go on a Letter Hunt. Can they identify letters or make a word with the letters they find?

Touch and Tell

Place a magnetic letter in a sock. Challenge children to reach into the sock and identify the letter by feeling it.

Building Words

Demonstrate how to build words with magnetic letters. (This is really cool on an overhead projector!)

Letter Monster

Color and cut out the monster face (see the illustration on the right). Glue the face to a bag or small trash can with a swing top. Ask the children to "feed the monster" all the letters they know, the letters in their names, all the red letters, and so on.

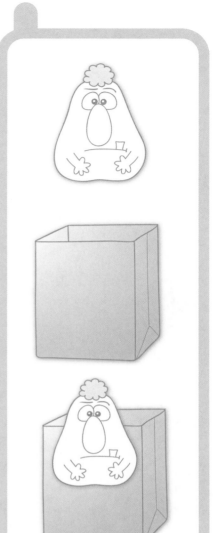

Letter Tree

Read the book *Chicka Chicka Boom Boom* by Bill Martin, Jr. and John Archambault to the children. Let the children help make a classroom letter tree using a large, empty metal coffee can or vegetable can, brown or gold spray paint (adult only), two or three different shades of green felt, a small piece of brown felt, a magnetic strip, and craft glue. Away from the children, spray paint the can gold or brown. (**Note:** Spray paint the can while children are not in the room and allow it to dry.) Cut out nine palm fronds from felt using the pattern on the following page. Glue the palm fronds as shown and attach a magnetic strip to the bottom of them. Cut out several coconuts from the brown felt and glue on top of the palm fronds. Turn the can upside down and place the palms on top to create a tree. Attach magnetic letters to the side of the can.

1. Cut out nine palm leaves from green felt.

2. Glue the ends of the leaves together as shown to make a cluster.

3. Cut out three coconuts from brown felt. Glue them to the middle of the cluster.

4. Attach a piece of magnetic tape to the back of the palms and stick on top of the can.

palm

coconut

Hint! You can make a similar tree and letters out of paper for your bulletin board. Or, place a large tree branch in a can of sand and hang letters on it.

Children place the letters in their name on the tree, attach the letters they can recognize, attach letters that are all the same color, make words, and so on. When they are finished playing with the tree, they can turn the can over and place the palms and letters into the can.

Pattern for Letter Tree

1. Cut out nine palm leaves from green felt.
2. Glue the ends of the leaves together as shown to make a cluster.
3. Cut out three coconuts from brown felt and glue them to the middle of the cluster.
4. Attach a piece of magnetic tape to the back of the palms and stick on top of the can.

Who Let the Letters Out?

Cut out a doghouse from poster board using the pattern below. Attach a piece of magnetic tape to the back of the doghouse and place it on a magnetic board or cookie sheet. Let the children take turns putting letters in the doghouse and then asking who let the letter out. For example, if the child puts an M in the doghouse, he would say, "Who let the M out? /m/ /m/ /m/ /m/ /m/." Encourage the children to think of words that begin with the sound.

CHAPTER 7

Letter Games: Games That Teach!

If it's not fun, why do it? Children are much more likely to be interested in something if it is in a game format. They like action-packed, hands-on, and social activities with friends. Repetition is a key to learning, which is part of what make these simple games that children want to play over and over so successful.

Quick Games

The following games are quick and fun. The children will be excited, so they won't even realize how much they are learning as they play!

Skill Development

Children will:

- increase alphabet knowledge
- improve social skills

Swat It!

Write letters on the chalkboard. Give one child an unused flyswatter and call out a letter. Can she "swat" the letter?

Boom!

Write letters on index cards. Write the word "BOOM!" on several cards with a bright colored marker. Shuffle the cards. Children call out the letters as you show them. When the "BOOM!" card appears, they jump up and shout, "Boom!" As a variation, change the word "boom" to a seasonal word or theme-related word. For example, in November you could use a picture of a turkey. When the turkey card appears, children jump up and "gobble." For a dinosaur unit, put dinosaur stickers on several cards. Children jump up, growl, and stomp like a dinosaur when it appears.

Letter Worm

Draw the face of a worm on an 8" circle similar to the one shown. Cut out 26 5" circles from construction paper and write a different letter of the alphabet on each. Pass out letters to the children. Place the worm's head on the floor. One at a time, the children come up, say their letter, and place it on the worm. If they do not know their letter, they can ask a friend.

- Challenge the children to place the letters in alphabetical order! "Who has A? What comes next?"

Active Games

Children need lots of activity and opportunities to run around. When the weather is poor, and the children are stuck indoors, try using some of the following active games to help them release their pent-up energy! These active games will get children moving, learning, and having fun at the same time.

Skill Development

Children will:

- increase alphabet knowledge
- improve social skills

Musical Letters

Write letters on paper plates. You will need as many plates as there are children in the class. Put the plates on the floor in a circle. Start the music and the children walk around the circle. Stop the music and each child picks up the plate closest to her. Call on different children to identify their letters. If they don't know their letters, they can "phone a friend" (hold up their hand by their ear and pretend to call someone) to ask for help. After they put their plates back on the floor, start the music to continue the game.

Letters in My Basket

Place letter cards or magnetic letters in a basket. Have the children sit in a circle on the floor. Choose a child to be "IT." IT skips around the circle with the basket full of letters as the children sing:

A tisket, a tasket,
There are letters in my basket.
I'll drop one behind a friend
And see if they can name it.

IT drops a letter behind one child. That child identifies the letter and then exchanges places with IT. If the child can't name the letter, she can ask the other children to help her.

Twister

Write letters on paper plates and place six to nine on the floor as shown. Have one child at a time come up and follow the directions as you call them out. For example, "Put your left hand on the W. Put your right foot on the C." Make directions increasingly complex for added fun!

Stomp!

Place large, cutout letters on the floor. Help the children take off their shoes. Two or three children at a time play the game. Call out a letter. Who can be the first to "stomp" on it?

Red Rover

Divide the class into two teams and have them stand 10'–20' apart facing each other. Give each child a cutout letter to hold in her hands. Let teams take turns saying, "Red Rover, Red Rover, send (name a letter) right over." The child holding that letter walks to the other team. Then the other team gets to call a letter over.

Snowballs

To make snowballs, write letters on scrap paper and wad them up. Divide the class into two teams and have them stand in two lines about 25' apart. Give each child a "snowball" and call out, "Let it snow!" The children throw their snowballs at the opposite team. Children pick up the snowballs, open them, identify the letter, then wad it back up, and throw it at the other team.

Games with Teacher-Made Props

The following games require that you make a few simple props beforehand.

Skill Development

Children will:

- increase alphabet knowledge
- develop social skills
- improve visual skills and visual matching
- practice motor skills
- develop phonological awareness

Letter Poke and Peek

Cut out a turtle from green poster board (or white poster board and color with a green crayon) using the pattern below. Punch holes around the turtle. Write a different uppercase letter next to each punched hole on one side of the turtle and the matching lowercase letters on the other side of the turtle. Two children play this game. One child holds the turtle, sticks a straw through the hole, and names the letter. The second child sits opposite the first child and checks her response.

Hint! Adapt this game to any seasonal shape or object.

Letter Socks

Cut socks out of construction paper using the pattern on the right. Write uppercase letters on some of the socks and lowercase letters on the other socks. Place the socks in a box or basket. Have children find the socks that match and clip them together with a clothespin or paper clip. Adapt the number of socks to the ability of the children. You might want to begin with five pairs and increase the number of pairs as children become more proficient.

Hint! Tie a string between two chairs and have children "hang up" the socks.

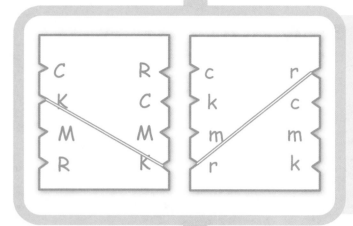

Stretch and Match

Hint! Make similar games for matching rhyming pictures, sounds, and so on.

Cut out rectangles with notches from cardboard using the pattern at left. Write matching letters on opposite sides as shown. On the back of the rectangle, draw lines to the letters that match. Have the children stretch rubber bands between like letters. They can turn the cards over and self-check.

Puzzle Pairs

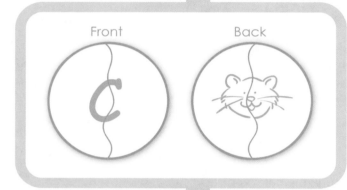

Front   Back

You will need paper plates to make this game. Write a letter on the left side of the plate and glue or draw a picture of an object that begins with that sound on the right side. Cut a puzzle design in the middle as shown. Invite the children to mix up the puzzle pieces and try to match beginning sounds and objects. This is a self-check game that ensures successful repetition.

- Cut paper plates into thirds. Write the uppercase letter in one section, the lowercase letter in another section, and glue a picture that begins with the letter in the third. Have children put them together.

- Use puzzle pairs for matching pictures that rhyme or words and pictures.

Egg Match

You will need plastic eggs and a permanent marker for this game. Write an uppercase letter on one half of the egg and the matching lowercase letter on the other half. Take the eggs apart and place them in a basket or box. Invite the children to match the letters as they put the eggs together.

- Let children place small objects (or pictures of the objects) that begin with the letters inside the eggs (for example, a small plastic frog inside the F egg).

- Write words (or children's names) on the outside of the egg. Cut out 1" squares, write the letters in the word on the pieces of paper, and put them inside the egg. Children remove the letters and put the squares together to make the word on the egg.

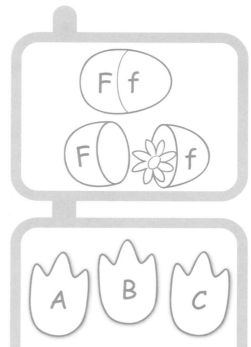

Dinosaur Feet

Cut out dinosaur feet from construction paper using the pattern below. If possible, laminate for durability. Write letters on the feet and scatter them around the room. Invite the children to take turns walking, hopping, or tiptoeing on the feet as they name the letters. Can the children put the feet in alphabetical order?

Beanbag Toss

Make a beanbag by placing a cup of small pebbles or beads in an old sock. Wrap a rubber band around the foot of the sock, and then fold the cuff back over the toe. Draw a grid on a large piece of poster board or bulletin board paper (three squares across and four squares down). Write different letters in each square. Have children stand behind a designated line and toss the beanbag. What letter does it land on? Can they think of a word that begins with the sound?

Fishing for Letters

Cut out fish from construction paper or fun foam using the pattern below. Write letters on the fish. Attach a paper clip to the mouth of each fish. Next, make a fishing pole from a wooden dowel or cardboard roller from a pants hanger. Tie a 24" piece of string to the end of the stick, and then tie a horseshoe magnet to the other end of the string. Scatter the fish on the floor. Invite the children to use the fishing pole to try to "catch" a fish. They can keep the fish if they can identify the letter on it.

Good Dog!

Cut out 25 dog bone shapes from a piece of poster board. Write letters on 20 of the bones, "Good dog!" on two of the bones, and "Woof!" on the other three bones. Mix up the bones and put them face down in a clean, plastic dog dish. The children sit in a circle and pass the bowl around. Each child selects a bone and names the letter. If the child selects "Good dog!" she pats her head and says, "Good dog!" If the child selects "Woof!" she gets down on the floor and barks like a dog. (Substitute a stuffed dog, if desired.)

- Adapt the number of letters and bones to the ability of your children. You could also ask them to make the sound of the letter or think of a word that starts with that sound.

Letter Sort

You will need 24 index cards and three paper lunch bags for this activity. Write the letter A on eight cards, B on eight cards, and C on eight cards. Write an A, B, or C on the lunch bags. Shuffle the cards and then have the children sort them into the correct bags. (You can use any letters of the alphabet for this activity.)

- Make a similar game where children sort letters that are curved (C, D, G), straight (I, L, T), or both.

- Make copies of letters in different fonts. Help the children sort the letters that are the same.

- Make a lotto sorting game from two 9" x 9" squares of poster board. Draw a grid with 3" squares on each piece of poster board. Write the same letters on both grids. Cut one apart to make nine pieces. Mix up the pieces, and then ask children to match them to the correct square.

Letter Shadows

Cut out two of each letter you want to use for this activity, one from black paper and the matching letter in a primary color. Glue the black letters on a poster board or file folder. Invite the children to try to match the colored letters with the "shadow" outline. Can they identify the letters?

- Make a placemat for each child using a similar technique. Cut out two of each letter in the child's name. Glue one copy to a 12" x 10" sheet of construction paper. Laminate or cover with clear contact paper. As children are waiting for snack, they can match the second set of letters to their placemat.

Letter Detectives

The following activities are memory games, which will help children improve their visual memory as well as their concentration and letter recognition.

Skill Development

Children will:

- increase alphabet knowledge
- improve visual memory

Missing Letter

Place four or five magnetic letters on a cookie sheet. Point to each letter as you name it. Ask the children to close their eyes. Remove one letter. When they open their eyes, have them hold up their thumb if they know which letter is missing. Let them all say the missing letter at the same time.

> **Hint!** You can also use felt letters on a flannel board for this activity.

Word Game

Write a child's name on the chalkboard. Read the letters together and ask the children to close their eyes. Erase one letter. When they open their eyes, can they identify the letter you erased?

> **Hint!** Use color words or other high frequency words for this activity.

Clues

Tell the children they are "detectives." Give them clues to describe letters. For example: "I'm looking for a letter that is made with a straight line and a curve. It comes near the beginning of the alphabet. It's a consonant. You hear it at the beginning of the words *dog, dad*, and *Danielle*. Who knows the mystery letter?"

Alphabet Books

Place sticky notes over letters in alphabet books. "What letter could it be?" Have children guess and then remove the sticky note.

CHAPTER 8

Write On! Pre-Writing Experiences to Get Children Ready to Write

Writing is a form of expressive language. Just as children begin speaking by babbling, they begin writing by scribbling. It is important to have writing materials available to children, and to encourage them to explore by making marks on the page. Eventually, children will learn that they can write what they say and they can read what they write! This wonderful literacy circle can begin by using some of the simple activities in this chapter. Children shouldn't be pushed, but they should be provided with the tools to move to the next level in their development.

Getting Ready to Write

Children will become more aware of directionality as you sing songs and play games that require them to discriminate between their left and right. Use air writing and invisible writing to create a larger image in the brain. As children explore writing letters, they will feel more confident and excited about writing independently.

Skill Development

Children will:

- learn left from right
- gain an interest in writing
- increase print knowledge

Left and Right

Tie a yarn bracelet around the child's right wrist or put a sticker on his right hand. Do the "Looby Loo," "Simon Says," "Go Bananas," and other games and songs where children must identify their left and right hand and other body parts. Show them how to make an "L" with the thumb and index finger on their left hand, and teach them this song to the tune of "Up on the Housetop."

> *This is my right hand, reach up high.*
> *This is my left hand, touch the sky.*
> *Right and left,*
> *Roll out of sight.*
> *Now I know my left and right.*

Sing the song faster, slower, louder, softer, and so on.

Cotton Ball Grip

Give each child a cotton ball to hold in his hand when he writes. Demonstrate how to put your pinky and ring finger to "sleep" on the cotton ball before you pick up a pencil. They will naturally use the correct grip!

- Provide children with a variety of writing instruments to choose from, such as fat pencils, skinny pencils, pencil grips, pens, colored pencils, and so on.

Invisible Writing

Use some of the following multi-sensory strategies when introducing writing. You will need to reverse the movements or turn around while demonstrating these in front of the class.

Skill Development
Children will:
- increase alphabet knowledge
- practice small motor skills
- develop an interest in writing

Air Writing
Write letters in the air using your index finger and middle finger. Keep your elbow stiff.

Clap and Clasp Writing
Have children clap their hands together and clasp their fingers. Practice making lines, shapes, and letters in the air using clasped hands.

Body Writing
Use elbows, tongues, noses, feet, and other body parts to write letters in the air.

Tummy Writing
Try "tummy writing!" Have the children lie on the floor on their tummies. They can extend their arms and trace giant letters on the floor.

Flashlight
Turn off the lights and make letters on the wall or ceiling with a flashlight. As a variation, tape letters to the ceiling. Invite the children to lie on their backs and shine a flashlight on the letters as you sing alphabet songs.

Palm Writing
The children write letters on their palms. Hold up one palm and trace letters with the index finger from the other hand.

Pass the Letter

Have children sit on the floor in a circle facing each other's backs. Start by tracing a letter on the first child's back as she says, "This is an H." That child traces the H on the next child's back as she says, "This is an H." Children continue to "pass" the letter around the circle as they write it on each other's backs.

Partner Writing

Let children write letters on their partner's backs. Can the partners guess the letters their friends write?

Floor Letters

Divide children into groups and challenge them to lie on the floor and create letters with their bodies.

Disappearing Letters

Write giant letters with chalk on the board. Children dip a sponge in water and trace over the letters as they erase them.

Water Writing

Draw letters on the playground using a paintbrush and a bucket of water. Children "paint" letters on the sidewalk, building, or playground equipment, and then watch them disappear.

Wipe-Off Board

Make individual wipe-off boards for the children by purchasing shower stall laminate at a building supply store. Ask a store employee to cut it into 8" x 10" sections. Give children dry-erase markers for writing and old socks for erasing!

■ ■ ■ ■ ■ ■
Hint! You could also provide a white plastic plate, dry-erase marker, and a paper towel eraser.

This Is the Way We Write the Song

Skill Development

Children will:

- practice pre-writing
- develop small motor skills
- see print connection
- practice left to right orientation

Children will have fun developing their small motor skills as they sing the traditional song "This Is the Way We Wash Our Clothes."

Have the children practice making the motions below in the air using their fingers. Give each child a sheet of paper and to practice making the strokes.

This is the way we wash the clothes,
Wash the clothes, wash the clothes.
This is the way we wash the clothes
So early in the morning.

This is the way we iron the clothes…
This is the way we scrub the floor…
This is the way we mend the clothes…
This is the way we sweep the floor…
This is the way we bake our bread…
This is the way we smile and sing…

○○○○	Go 'round the mulberry bush
| | | | | | | |	Wash the clothes
= = = =	Iron the clothes
V V V V	Scrub the floor
X X X X	Mend the clothes
∧ ∧ ∧ ∧	Sweep the floor
☺ ☺ ☺ ☺	Bake our bread
∪∪∪∪∪	Smile and sing

Hint! Children can also do this using chalk on the sidewalk, a wet sponge on the chalkboard, or with sand in a sand tray.

Letter Rhymes

Sing or say the rhymes below as children make the letters in the air. Focus on one letter at a time and add new letters when the children are learning about them. Remember, when modeling this in front of the class, reverse the movements or turn around so children see the proper letter formation.

Skill Development

Children will:

- increase alphabet knowledge
- develop print knowledge
- practice small motor skills

Uppercase Letter Rhymes

(Tune: "Skip to My Lou") by Dr. Holly Karapetkova

Letters are made from circles and lines,
Pushes, slants, each letter looks fine.
Make them as we sing this song.
It's easy when you join along.

Slant, slant, push in between.
Slant, slant, push in between.
Slant, slant, push in between
To make the letter A.

Pull straight down two humps on the right.
Pull straight down two humps on the right.
Pull straight down two humps on the right
To make the letter B.

C—Circle round and then you stop…
D—Long straight line and half a circle…
E—Pull straight down, then push, push, push…
F—A tall line, push at the top and middle…
G—Circle round, stop, and then push in…
H—Pull, pull, push in between…
I—Pull, little push at the top and bottom…
J—Pull down, make a hook, put a hat on top…
K—Straight line, slant in, and out again…
L—A long line and push on the ground…
M—Two straight lines, two slants in between…
N—Pull, pull, slant top to bottom…

O—Circle round then back to the top…
P—Pull straight down, then a hump from the top…
Q—Make a circle then a small slanted line…
R—Pull straight down, hump and slant…
S—Curve up and down, then curve down and up…
T—Straight line down, push at the top…
U—Pull down curve then back to the top…
V—Slant, slant, meet at the bottom…
W—Slant down, up, down and up…
X—Two slanted lines that cross in the middle…
Y—Two small slants on a straight line…
Z—Push right, slant down and push right again…

You can write your ABCs.
You can write your ABCs.
You can write your ABCs.
Give yourself a big smiley! (draw a pretend smiley face in the air)

Rhyme to Write Lowercase Letters

(Tune: "On Top of Old Smokey") by Dr. Holly Karapetkova
First make a circle, then a short straight line.
That's a lowercase a, and it looks just fine.

Now make a long line with a circle on the ground.
And you've made a b with the /b/ /b/ /b/ sound.

Letter c is like a circle, but it doesn't close up.
For cotton candy and carrots and cups.

Small d has a circle that sits on the ground
And a straight line on the right, for dog, dance, and down.

E starts with a straight line from the side you see
Then curves up around and down, that's lowercase e.

Letter f has a hook that curves at the top
Then a long line straight down and a short one across.

For g make a circle and a hook stretching down.
Like the trunk of an elephant sweeping the ground.

H has a long line and a hump on the right.
It's a letter with happiness, health and height.

For I make a short line, then a dot overhead
For words like important, inch, if, and instead.

Letter j has a long hook that stretches below
And a dot on the top for jump, joy, and joke.

When you make a long line, and two short ones slant out
It's lowercase k without a doubt!

Letter l's very simple, just one long straight line.
Keep your pen on the paper and you'll make l just fine.

Now make a short line and two round humps.
Your m's like two mountains, or mole hills or mumps.

N's just like m, with one hump less—
For never and no one and nickel and nest.

O is a circle, entirely round.
There isn't a straight line or edge to be found.

P starts with a straight line that goes down below.
Then a small circle just like letter o.

Q is like p, but the line's on the right
And kicks up at the end, q's quite out of sight!

Now make a short line, entirely straight
With a hook on the top—your r is first rate!

Letter s is swirley, it swerves and it bends;
Curve up around, slant down, then curve up again.

T has a straight line that's medium-sized
Then a shorter one crosses from side to side.

U is like n turned upside down;
Make a curve with your pencil, then a straight line down.

V has two straight lines, and both of them slant.
They meet at the bottom—how about that!

W is two v's stuck side by side;
W is for welcome, with arms open wide.

Now make two slanted lines, at the middle
    they cross
For X-men and x-ray, your x marks the spot.

Letter y has two lines that touch, you know
A short one and a long one that stretches
    below.

Z makes zigzags for zany and Zen;
Straight across the top, slant down, then
    straight out again.

You've made all the letters. Way to go!
You'll be writing words before you know!

Clipboard Writing

Skill Development

Children will:

- practice invented writing
- develop print knowledge

Letter Clipboards

Children will love walking around the room and writing with their very own clipboards. Let each child use markers or crayons to decorate a 12" x 10" piece of corrugated cardboard. Attach a butterfly clip at the top, and insert paper.

Letter Hunt

Encourage the children to walk around the room and copy letters on their paper.

Write the Room

Children copy environmental print that they can read in the classroom.

Observations

Ask the children to look out the window and draw pictures of what they see. Or, if possible, take a nature walk and have them "record data."

Blocks

Invite the children to pretend to be construction supervisors in the Block Center. Have them sketch structures they have built or are going to build.

Rest and Doodle

At Quiet Time, let children doodle, scribble, draw, or write on their clipboards.

Write On with Blank Books

Children will be excited about "writing" when you provide them with some of the following books. These books are different from regular blank books, they will inspire the children to use them and write in them.

Skill Development

Children will:

- develop small motor skills
- demonstrate emergent writing

Fold-and-Tear Book

Fold two sheets of paper in half. Make tears (or snips) about a thumbnail apart down the fold. Bend one tab forward, then the next backward, and so on to bind the pages together.

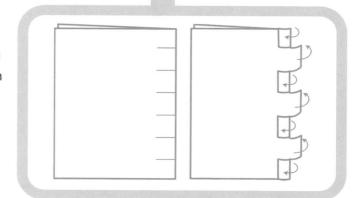

- Use a white sheet of paper and a colored sheet of paper and it will really look like a book!

Invite children to use fold-and-tear books for:

- retelling a story

- illustrating a nursery rhyme

- writing a journal ("Draw what you did at school today.")

- creating a sticker book

- gluing environmental print ("Cut out words you can read.")

- creating a take-home book to make with parents ("I like…" "I can…")

- making a letter book ("Draw objects that begin with the sound.")

- making a science book (Provide library books about a topic and let them do "research" and make their own book about it.)

- blank books to use in the Writing Center, Dramatic Play Center, and so on.

Brochure

To make a brochure (or tri-fold), roll a sheet of paper into a burrito and "smash" it flat.

Use brochures to:

- tell the beginning, middle, and end of a story

- make a follow-up to a field trip

- make an "all about me" brochure

- sort pictures, letters, words, and anything else

- draw a body (different parts on each fold)

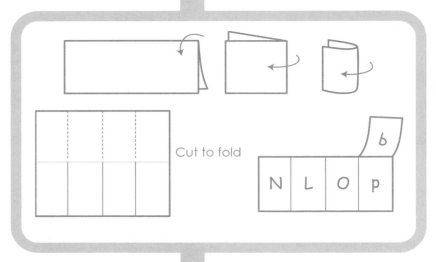

Cut to fold

Flip Book

Fold a sheet of paper in half lengthwise. Fold in half again, and then again. Open. Cut halfway up on the creased lines as shown. Fold in half again and open the flaps. (Children call this a garage door book!)

Use flip books for:

- matching uppercase and lowercase letters

- collecting pictures that rhyme

- matching words and pictures

- illustrating opposites

- matching mother and baby animals

- creating "before" and "after" pictures

- matching numerals and sets

- outlining sequence of a story

Step Book

Layer two sheets of paper about 1" apart as shown. Fold backwards to create a step book with four layers. Staple at the top.

- You can use additional sheets of paper to make more steps.

- Use different colors of paper to create a rainbow book.

Step books work well for:

- four seasons

- days of the week

- number books

- repetitive songs and stories

- "How to" books

Folded Book

Fold a sheet of paper in half and then into fourths.

Children can make this book and use it for:

- making cards for friends

- writing in blank books in centers

- recording letters and objects that begin with a sound

- making concept books (colors, shapes, numbers)

Craft Stick Book

You will need paper, a craft stick, rubber band, and hole punch to make this book. Fold two sheets of paper in half and cut along the folded line. Stack these and fold in half again. Hole punch on the folded side about 1 ½" from each end. Push one end of the rubber band through one hole and insert the end of the popsicle stick through the loop. Push the other end of the rubber band through the other hole and insert the other end of the craft stick through that loop.

Children use craft stick books for:

- autograph books

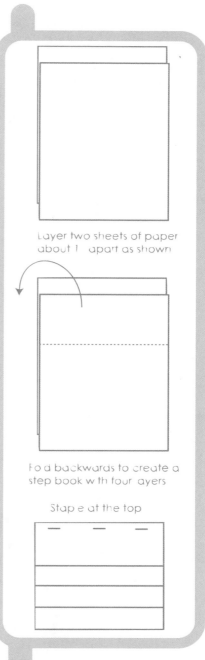

Layer two sheets of paper about 1" apart as shown

Fold backwards to create a step book with four layers

Staple at the top

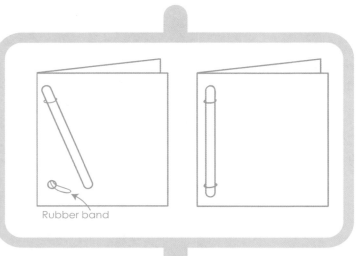

- letter/ABC books

- illustrating nursery rhymes

- predictable books ("I like…" "I can…" "I eat…")

- journals

- Substitute a real stick for the craft stick and use for a nature book, a crayon for a color book, or a plastic spoon for a cookbook.

- Fold three sheets of paper in half to make a larger book. Use a novelty pencil for the binding.

House Book

Fold a sheet of paper in half lengthwise. Open. Bring the upper left corner to the center crease. Bring the upper right corner to the center crease. Fold up the bottom edge to create a "house."

Children can use house books to make a book about their families, to draw a map of their house, to illustrate a story that takes place in a house ("The Three Bears," "The Three Little Pigs," and so on), and for following directions. ("Draw a ball in the attic of the house, two windows on the outside, a mouse in the basement," and so on.)

Book Box

Ask families to send in an empty cereal box for their child. Away from the children, spray paint boxes with gold or silver paint (adult only). Let them dry. Invite the children to decorate their boxes with glitter pens and stickers and use them as "treasure boxes" for storing the books that they make at school. Help each child write his name on the side panel and store them on a bookshelf. Whenever children make books in class, have them add the books to their boxes. They can get out their book boxes at quiet time. Let children take them home over holidays, school vacations, and at the end of the school year so they will always have a book to read!

Accordion Books

Fold a sentence strip in half, quarters, and then eighths. Now fold back and forth like a fan as shown. (You can also cut long strips of paper to make an accordion book.)

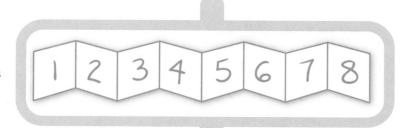

Have the children use accordion books for:

- writing the letters in their names

- drawing the sequence of a song or story

- making a number book

- drawing the life cycle of a butterfly, frog, or other animal or insect

Tag-Along Book

Fold a sheet of construction paper in half. Fold two sheets of white paper in half and insert inside the folded construction paper. Punch two holes in the creased edge and twist a pipe cleaner through the holes to make a handle. The book can "tag along" wherever the children carry it!

Tag-along books are fun to bring on a nature walk or field trip, as a take-home journal over a holiday or weekend, or as a concept book (clothes, colors, letters).

Gift Bag Book

Cut the front and back off a gift bag. These will be the front and back covers for a class book. Let the gift bag serve as the theme for the book. For example, a bag with hearts could be "Things We Love." Cut white paper the size of the bag and give a sheet to each child. Have them illustrate something that fits the theme of the book (for a theme of love, they could draw their parents, a pet, a favorite food or book, and so on). Staple the children's drawings between the front and back covers of the book.

Baggie Book

Give each child four sandwich-size resealable bags and paper cut to fit inside the bags (5"–5 ½" squares). Children draw pictures on the paper, insert the paper in the bags, and zip shut. Tape the children's baggies outside the zipper to create a water-tight seal. These are perfect for reading in the bathtub!

Children can use baggie books for storing photographs, collecting leaves and natural objects, and to make "All About Me" books.

ABC Books

The following books are child-made and focus on the alphabet.

Skill Development

Children will:

- increase alphabet knowledge
- practice motor skills
- improve visual tracking and skills
- develop print knowledge

"Y" is for Yolonda!

■ ■ ■ ■ ■ ■ ■
Hint! Invite the children to make the correct letter form over their body representations using a highlighter marker.

Alpha-Body Book

Encourage each to child use his body to make the letter that his first or last name begins with. Take a photo of the child. The child glues his photo to a piece of construction paper and writes a sentence underneath, such as "Y is for Yolanda!" You might need to write the sentence for the child.

■ Divide children into groups of three or four and ask them to lie on the floor to create different letters. Take photos and put them together to make a class book.

I Can Read from A to Z

Take 26 large sheets of paper and write a different letter on each page. Put the pages between two pieces of construction paper to make a book entitled "I Can Read My ABCs." Hole punch and bind with book rings. Invite children to bring in words from food labels, store circulars, catalogs, and other environmental print that they can read. As children bring in their words, help them match the first letter with the same letter in the book and glue their word on that page. When the book is finished, ask children to find different words they can read.

■ Make an alphabet book with candy wrappers. (This works especially well right after Halloween!) Call it "My Sweet ABCs" and glue candy wrappers on the appropriate pages.

Eat from A Through Z

Assign each child a letter of the alphabet and a day to bring snack. On the child's day, he should bring a food that begins with his assigned sound. For example, if the child has the letter C, he could bring in carrots, crackers, cheese, cookies, or any other snack food that begins with a C. **Note:** This will require a note home to families identifying the child's letter, day of his assigned snack, and guidelines for acceptable foods to bring in.

Take a photograph of the child with his snack and make an ABC book for your classroom. For example, if the child brings in bananas for B, take a photo of the child holding a banana. Glue the photo on a page and write, "Brendan brought bananas."

Hint! This would be a great project for families to make for their children at a workshop.

Alphabet Fold-Out Book

To make this book, you will need two sentence strips for each child. Fold each strip in half, then quarters, and then eighths. Open up and accordion fold back and forth. Tape the two sections together. Since you will only need 14 folds, cut off the last two sections and discard. Write "My Alphabet Book" on the first section. Next, invite the children to write the letters of the alphabet on each section as shown from A–M. Turn over and complete the alphabet from N–Z. Help them write "The End" on the last section. Fold and tie a ribbon around the book.

■ You could use this technique to make a counting book.

Alphabet Art Book

Write large letters of the alphabet on paper. Give each child a letter and challenge him to create a picture around his letter. For example, he could make a tree from the letter Y, a person from the letter A, and so on. Ask the children questions to get them started. "What does your letter look

like? Does it remind you of something? Can you use your crayons to turn it into that object?" Challenge them to "camouflage" their letter. Put their drawings together to make a book. Can they find the letter hidden in each picture?

■ Challenge older children to turn their letter into an object that begins with the sound their letter makes.

I Spy Alphabet Book

Give each child a sheet of paper and ask him to write all the letters he can. Put all of the papers between two pieces of construction paper and bind together with book rings. Write "I Spy Letters!" on the front cover. Select one letter on each page and write, "I spy _____!" Give the children a "magnifying glass" (pipe cleaner twisted into a circle) or bubble wand to find and frame the letter.

■ You can make a similar book by making copies of a sheet of paper with all the letters scrambled up on it. Write a different letter at the top of each page (for example, "Where is F?") on each page for the children to find.

Alphabet Journal

Use special events, activities, favorite songs, books, and so on during the school year to stimulate journal writing for each letter. Have children write the significant letter at the top of the page and illustrate it. Then ask them to write (or dictate) about the event. Save and bind as an "end of year" memory!

For example, the letter A, a child could write or draw about an apple tasting day in the fall or a big art project; for the letter B, he might write or draw about his birthday, his school bus, favorite books, or a special block center creation. Do this for each letter of the alphabet.

See and Sign

Enlarge copies of the sign language alphabet (see page 79). Put a different letter and sign on each page. Invite different children to illustrate something that begins with that sound. Bind the pages together to make a class book. Encourage the children to reproduce the signs on each page as they read the book.

■ ■ ■ ■ ■ ■
Hint! You can also photograph children's hands making the signs and use the photos for your alphabet book.

More Than ABCs

Make alphabet books that relate to different themes, seasons, holidays, or concepts you are working on. For example, pets, favorite foods, transportation, Halloween, Winter, Things We Are Thankful For, and so on.

■ You could also involve families in making an alphabet book. Give each family a sheet of paper with a letter on it. Ask them to cut out words or pictures of things that begin with the letter. Put their pages together to make a book for your class.

Feel the Letters

Make letters from sensory materials. For example, cut out letters from sandpaper, colorful felt and fun foam, fake fur, textured fabrics, and any other textured material you have. Have the children glue the letters to heavy paper. Make a cover and bind the pages together to make a book that children can "feel" as they read!

Other ideas include:

■ Make letters from plastic needlepoint canvas. This plastic material looks like screening and can be purchased at most craft stores. Have the children make rubbings of these letters by placing a sheet of paper on top and rubbing with a crayon.

■ Write letters in glue and sprinkle with glitter or colored sand. Let dry.

■ Make letter outlines with glue, and then place yarn on top. Let dry.

■ Glue cotton balls to letter outlines.

Hint! Most of these materials can be cut out on a die-cut machine.

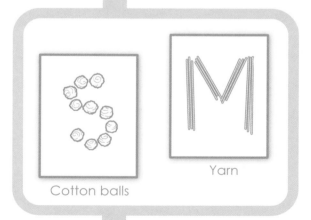

Cotton balls

Yarn

CHAPTER 9

Letters to Send Home: Strategies to Involve Families

Newsletters

If you want to make a significant difference in children's lives, then you must also reach out to the children's families and teach them as well. The more involved families are in their children's education, the more successful their children will be in school.

Here are some activities that will help families feel welcome and show them that they are a vital part of your program:

- Give children take-home projects to complete with their families.
- Start a monthly reading calendar.
- Send home copies of "Letter Limericks," songs, and rhymes (see pages 123–126).
- Have family meetings and open houses.
- Plan family fun nights (storytellers, movies, skating, potlucks).
- Invite families in to watch their children's plays and other programs.
- Provide a family resource library (books, DVDs, journals, and magazines).
- Hold seminars around topics of interest (nutrition, discipline, reading).
- Schedule individual family conferences and make phone calls.
- Encourage families to volunteer in the classroom (make materials, help with cooking activities or art projects, chaperone field trips, and so on).
- Invite guest readers (parents, grandparents, or other family members) to come in and read to the class.
- Send home school newsletters.
- Send home community newsletters about events outside school.
- Have an "open door" policy that families are always welcome in your classroom.

On the following pages are newsletters that you can send home to families. Most of the suggested activities are simple, fun, and will develop the children's language skills. Feel free to change the letters to meet the special needs of your population. If the children's families are not English speakers, for example, then it will be important to have the letters translated.

Read, Read, Read!

Dear Families,

You've heard it before, and I'll say it again. **You are your child's first and most important teacher!** Over the next few weeks I'll be sending home letters with suggestions for how you can help your child at home. You'll discover how much fun reading, talking, singing, and playing with your child can be! And you'll be laying the groundwork for a lifetime of learning and a love of reading.

The best way to help your child learn to read is to read, read, read to him or her!

1. Model reading in front of your child. Read in front of your child often. Read the newspaper, directions on recipes, labels on clothing, and street signs. Show your child the importance of reading, and also the pleasure you get from reading.

2. Set aside a special time each day to read with your child. It might be right before bed, or you could wake your child up each morning with a story.

3. Point your finger under the words as you read them.

4. Talk about the title of the book, the author, illustrator, and so on. Ask questions. "Where does the story take place (the setting)?" "Who are the characters?" "Could this really happen or is it a pretend story?" Do this in a fun way.

5. Take your child to the library. Help your child get his or her own library card and encourage him or her to take responsibility for books.

6. Create a special basket or shelf in your home where you keep books and magazines for your child to read. You might also want to keep a backpack filled with books in your car.

Happy reading!

Talk, Talk, Talk!

Dear Families,

Oral language is the foundation of literacy. Children with good verbal skills are generally better readers. Here are some simple things you can do to improve talking and listening at home.

1. Turn off the radio or CD player in your car. Talk about your day or just listen to your children talk.

2. Turn off your televsion! Limit television viewing to 30 minutes a day. When your child does watch, watch the programs with your child and talk about what is going on. Ask questions. "Who is your favorite character?" "Is it real or pretend?" "What do you think will happen next?"

3. Eat meals together. Try to eat at least one meal a day as a family. Turn off the radio, TV, and cell phone and you'll be amazed at how talking will increase.

4. Model correct language for your child. If your child says something incorrectly, don't reprimand him or her. Simply repeat it correctly so your child hears how it should be said.

5. Talk about what you see as you drive down the road or what you are doing as you prepare a meal. The more your child hears you talk, the more your child will want to talk.

6. Listen, listen, listen! Stop what you are doing and look your child in the eyes when he or she talks to you. Demonstrate to your child that what he or she has to say is important to you.

Happy talking!

Newsletter # 3

Sing, Sing, Sing!

Dear Families,

You don't have to be a great singer to enjoy singing with your child. Music is a powerful way to help children get ready to read.

1. What songs do you remember from your own childhood? Sing those to your child.

2. Ask your child to teach you a song that he or she has learned at school.

3. Check out children's recordings from the library. These are great to listen to as you do chores around the house or travel in the car.

4. Make up motions for songs. You can dance, clap, jump, patty cake, or do other movements.

5. Can't think of a song to sing? You'll probably remember some of these!

Alphabet Song
The Bear Went over the
  Mountain
BINGO
The Eensy Weensy Spider
The Farmer in the Dell
Hickory, Dickory, Dock
Hush, Little Baby
If You're Happy and You
  Know It
I've Been Working on the
  Railroad
London Bridge Is Falling
  Down

The Mulberry Bush
Old MacDonald
Pop! Goes the Weasel
Rain, Rain, Go Away
Ring Around the Rosie
Row, Row, Row Your Boat
She'll Be Coming 'Round the
  Mountain
Skip to My Lou
This Old Man
Twinkle, Twinkle, Little Star
Yankee Doodle
You Are My Sunshine
The Wheels on the Bus

Happy singing!

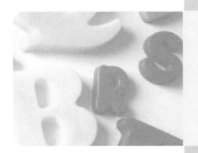

Rhyme, Rhyme, Rhyme!

Dear Families,

Knowing phonological awareness (rhyme, rhythm, and alliteration) is one of the best predictors of reading success. Your parents or grandparents probably didn't know it, but the nursery rhymes they said to you as a child were actually getting you ready to read!

1. Tell your child nursery rhymes as you help him or her get dressed, buckle your child in a car seat, or take a walk.

2. Act out nursery rhymes with your child. Hold hands and pretend to be "Jack and Jill," or jump over the moon and play your fiddle as in "Hey, Diddle, Diddle."

3. Sing nursery rhymes to the tune of "100 Bottles of Pop on the Wall" or "Yankee Doodle." Believe it or not, most rhymes can be sung to these two tunes!

4. Clap your hands to the rhythm of nursery rhymes.

5. Visit these websites to learn nursery rhymes and download some fun activities:

   www.curry.edschool.edu/go/wil/rimes_and_rhymes.htm
   www.kididdles.com
   www.rhymes.org.uk
   www.enchantedlearning.com

6. Children love silly words and rhymes, so make up your own rhyming games. For example, think of all the words that rhyme with your child's name.

7. Encourage your child to pick out words that rhyme as you read books or sing songs.

Happy rhyming!

Paper, Pencils, and Props

Dear Families,

Did you know that every time your child scribbles, he or she is setting the stage for future writing? Those little squiggles and lines will turn into letters, words, and stories one day! Here are some great tools that will give your child the opportunity to explore and develop small motor skills.

Note! Monitor the use of these materials and set rules and limits to where and when they can be used.

1. Keep pencils, pens, crayons, colored pencils, notepads, paper, spiral notebooks, and so on in a basket or old briefcase. The basket or briefcase makes the items portable. Encourage your child to play with the materials inside or outside.

2. Provide playdough, tape, watercolors, a hole punch, safety scissors, washable markers, construction paper, stickers, and other art media. You might want to store these materials in a plastic tub to make them convenient to get out and clean up.

3. Value your child's work by framing it or hanging it on the refrigerator.

4. Children enjoy drawing with chalk on the sidewalk. Or you could place a chalkboard in your garage or basement.

5. Save forms from magazines or junk mail for children to write on.

6. A magic slate, dry-erase board, seasonal pencil, note cards, and other props will engage your child in writing.

Happy writing!

Hint! These materials are great to give as birthday gifts.

Letters, Letters, Letters!

Dear Families,

Children are naturally interested in the letters they see in their world. You don't need flashcards or computer games; instead, take advantage of "teachable moments" with some of these ideas.

1. Point out letters in your home (on cereal boxes, household items, clothing, and appliances).

2. As you travel in the car, talk about letters on stores, restaurants, and signs.

3. Magnetic letters are a must! Children can play with these on a refrigerator or cookie sheet. Start with one or two letters and slowly add more. Point out the lines, circles, and unique configuration of each letter. Talk about the sound each letter makes. "This is the letter _____ and it makes the sound _____."

4. Look for crackers, cookies, or cereal in the shape of letters. You can also purchase letter-shaped cookie cutters, sponges, blocks, and other toys that will spark your child's interest in letters.

5. Talk about letters as you read to your child. "Can you find the letter ____ on this page?"

6. Write names of family members on index cards and attach them to the refrigerator or a poster. Talk about the different letters in each person's name.

7. Invite your child to dictate stories to you about their artwork or photographs you have taken. (Carefully write down what your child says and point to the words as you read them back to him or her.)

8. Write the words for objects in your child's room on sticky notes. Play a game where your child matches up the words with the objects.

Play, Play, Play!

Dear Families,

Have you ever heard the phrase, "play is a child's work"? This is so true! Children have their whole lives ahead of them to be adults and work, but only a short time to be young and have fun! The good news is that as you play with your child, you are actually laying the foundation for future learning. Children don't need more "stuff." What they want and need most is time and attention from you! The important thing is to follow your child's lead as you create special memories! Here are some "play activities" to get you started:

- Tell a joke.
- Sing a song.
- Play hide and seek.
- Hum a tune.
- Play a card game.
- Play a rhyming game.
- Play with playdough.
- Play follow the leader.
- Make silly faces in a mirror.
- Put on some music and dance.
- Make a puppet and put on a puppet show.
- Swing on a swing.
- Sit on the floor together and build something with blocks.
- Blow bubbles.
- Go outside and take a walk.
- Cut pictures out of magazines.
- Skip.
- Play a board game.
- Skate on paper plates.
- Make a wish on a star.
- Jump or hop as long as you can.
- Play a memory game.
- Cook something together.
- Work a puzzle.
- Make a band of pots and pans.
- Play "I spy."
- Draw a picture or color in a coloring book.
- Go to the library.
- Make a card for someone.

Happy playing!

Hint! Write these suggestions on paper and cut them into strips. Place the strips in a sack. Let your child choose a strip and then do that activity together.

Involving Families in Their Children's Learning

The following ideas will further involve families in their children's learning. Encourage families to help their children with the following activities.

Skill Development

Children will:

- develop alphabet knowledge
- practice oral language
- increase home/school connection
- develop phonological awareness

Hint! The first letter to send home should be the letter the child's name starts with. Continue sending home letters that relate to classroom activities. For example, send home a "P" when you go to the pumpkin patch, or an "A" when you do apple tasting.

Hint! It will take about a month for this lunchbox to circulate home with all the children in your classroom. Change the contents each month to relate to different classroom skills and themes. For example, in February you could have pink playdough and a heart shaped cookie cutter, envelopes and paper cut into hearts, a sewing card of a heart, eraser hearts to count and sort, and a small package of candy hearts to eat.

Refrigerator Letters and Words

Cut out letters from poster board. You may want to use a die-cut machine, if available. Give each child a set of letters to decorate. Provide crayons, markers, stickers, or glitter pens. Help them attach a piece of magnetic tape to the back of each letter. Send the letters home with the children, along with a note to families, suggesting that they talk about the letter, help their child find similar letters around the house, use the letters on a refrigerator or cookie sheet, and so on.

Ask the children to bring in labels from snack foods, fast food bags, toys, and other items they like. Print "I" on one index card and "like" on a second card. Demonstrate how to place the cards on the floor (I like _____) with their labels. Model pointing to the words and reading the sentences. Let children trade labels with friends. Attach magnetic tape to the back of the words and labels and send them home for the children to use on their refrigerator.

Letter Lunchbox

You will need an old metal lunchbox for this project. Place magnetic letters, small alphabet books, playdough, stencils, blank paper, scissors, colored pencils, and similar items in the lunch box. Also include a small healthy snack, such as raisins, crackers, or a small bag of pretzels. You might also include a comment card for the families. Put in a note to the families explaining how to use the materials and tell them their child can have the snack after he or she has played with the letters. Choose one child each day to take home the "letter lunchbox." The next day, ask the child to share what he or she did with the lunchbox.

Monthly Reading Calendar

Create a reading calendar each month similar to the one below. Send home a calendar at the beginning of each month along with a note to families to read to their child daily for at least 10 minutes. The child colors in one section of the calendar each day. When families return the completed calendars at the end of each month, save them in the children's portfolios.

Letter Limericks

Read the following limericks to the children for a delightful listening activity. Read them over and over again, and encourage the children to join in on words they know or fill in rhyming words in the chants. Can they close their eyes and "see" the letter in their mind? Can they use invisible writing to make the letter in the air? Send home copies of the limericks after you introduce them for families to reinforce at home. Write the letter in large print (about ½ to ¾ of the page) and write the limerick underneath.

Letter Limericks by Holly Karapetkova

*The first is a letter called **A**
With straight lines in every way.
Two lines point up top,
To the bottom they drop,
And **a**nother crosses the way.*

*The second letter is **B**
For **b**aseball, **b**aby, and **b**each.
Straight line down the side,
Two humps on the right—
It looks like a fat **b**umble**b**ee!*

*After **B** comes **C**:
Cookies, **c**elery, and **c**heese!
Like a smile big and wide
Turned on its side
It's easy to make **C**, you see!*

***D** is a letter that's plump
Like a tummy with one round hump.
A long line straight **d**own,
Then go out and around
For **d**ig, **d**ive, **d**ip, and **d**ump.*

After **D** comes **E**.
It's shaped like a comb with three teeth.
One line down the side,
Three more to the right
For **e**choes, **e**ars, **e**yeballs, and **e**at.

F is the next letter to name.
It can bring with it **f**ortune and **f**ame.
Like **E** in design
Without the bottom line
But it gets along **f**ine all the same.

After **F** comes **G**,
Which is curvy and round just like **C**.
When you reach the end, stop,
Put a straight line across
And your **G** will **g**iggle with **g**lee!

H is a letter with pride.
It has two long straight lines side by side
Then **h**ip, **h**op, and **h**iggle
Put another 'cross the middle
And your **H** will **h**ave nothing to **h**ide!

I comes after that,
Eating **i**ce cream, and yet it's not fat.
One line stretches down,
One lies on the ground
And one goes on top—a flat hat!

Now **j**ump, **j**oke, and **j**uggle—it's **J**
With lines both curvy and straight.
The curve starts up top
Then like a hook drops
And the straight line **j**uts over the way.

The letter **K** has quite a **k**ick
With a spine as straight as a stick.
From the middle about
Two arms reach out
For **k**angaroos, **k**indness, and **k**ids!

After **K** comes **L**,
It's a **l**etter with **l**ots to tell.
One **l**ine heads straight down,

One sticks out on the ground
Like a chair with no **l**egs—how swell!

M is a letter with size,
Like two **m**ountains side by side.
Two straight lines on the end
Two others point in
Making **m**oms, **m**ilk, and **m**esses—oh, **m**y!

N is like **M,** only thinner.
It didn't eat quite as much dinner—
For **N**ick and **N**oelle
Two lines parallel
And a diagonal one 'cross the center.

O is entirely round—
Not a single straight line to be found.
Like a wide **o**pen mouth
Saying **o**ops! **o**h! or **o**uch!
It makes **o**ceans and **o**ranges abound.

The next of the letters is **P**
For **p**eople and **p**eanuts and **p**lease.
Let one straight line **p**rop
With a loop on the top
And you'll make lots of **p**umpkins and **p**eas.

Q comes next without fail
With **q**uarters, **q**uick **q**uestions, and **q**uails.
First a circle that's fat
Then like the back of a cat
A straight line sticks out like a tail.

R is ever so clever.
It's **P** and **K** blended together:
The top hoops about
The bottom leg kicks out—
For **r**unning and **r**eading, there's no better.

S is a letter with style
For **s**ummer, **s**unshine, and **s**miles.
Go up and around
Then back around down
Like a **s**nake that **s**lithers for miles.

T is terrific and true
*Standing **t**all as all **t**owers do.*
One straight line sits over,
The other points lower
*For **t**igers, **t**rees, and **t**ickles too.*

***U** comes right after **T**.*
*It also comes just before **V**.*
An upside down hump
A straight line it bumps:
***U**nicorn, **u**niverse, **u**nique.*

***V** is very healthy—it's true!*
*With **v**itamins and **v**egetables for you:*
Two straight lines point down
And meet at the ground
*For **v**acations and **v**iolins, too.*

***W** is just like two **V**s*
Stuck together—like twins, you see.
*With **w**hy, **w**hen, and **w**here?*
*And **w**ho **w**ill be there?*
***W** makes **w**ords **w**ork **w**ith ease.*

***X** is the letter that's next.*
*Not many words start with an **X**,*
*But **X** marks the spot*
With two straight lines that cross—
***X** is never quite what you expect.*

*The next-to-last letter is **Y***
*For **y**ears and **y**es, give it a try.*
*Like a small **V** that sits*
On top of a stick
*Reaching for the **y**ellow sun in the sky.*

***Z** comes last for a reason*
*Bringing **z**eal, **z**ap, and **z**est to all seasons.*
One straight line slants down
Then at foot and at crown
*Two other lines **z**ip—very pleasing!*

Letter Limerick Notebooks

Ask families to send in a three-ring binder or folder. As you focus on different letters, give the children the appropriate letter limerick (see Letter Limericks on pages 123–126) to hole punch and put in their binders. Use the notebook for some of the following activities:

- Put dots of glue on top of the letter and let dry. Children trace over the letter with their finger as they say the rhyme.

- Encourage children to draw pictures of objects whose names begin with the sound.

- Children practice writing the letter on the page using colored pencils, pens, or crayons.

- Provide different alphabet art media for children to use to decorate pages. For example, sponge print letters, use letter stamps, letter stickers, and so on.

- Ask the children to circle the letter in the rhyme with a highlighter.

- Invite the children to walk around the room and find that letter in a word. Can they write the word?

Have the children take home "Letter Limerick Notebooks" each weekend. Encourage families to read the limerick to their child. Can their child name the letter? Can they match the letter with an object in their home that starts with that sound? Can they find that letter in a book or on print in their home? Invite families to write comments in the notebooks before returning them to school the following Monday.

Appendix

References

Adams, M. J., Foorman, B., Lundberg, I., & Beeler, T. 1998. *Phonemic awareness in young children: A classroom curriculum*. Baltimore, MD: Paul H. Brookes.

Bredekamp, S., Copple, C., & Neuman, S. 1999. *Learning to read and write: Developmentally appropriate practices*. Washington, DC: National Association for the Education of Young Children.

Burns, S., Griffin, P., & Snow, C. 1999. *Starting out right*. Washington, DC: National Academy Press.

Chall, J. S. 1967. *Learning to read: The great debate*. New York: McGraw-Hill.

Clay, M. 1993. *An observation survey of early literacy achievement*. Portsmouth, NH: Heinemann.

Cunningham, P. 1995. *Phonics they use: Words for reading and writing*. Boston: Allyn and Bacon.

Durkin, D. 1981. *Getting started reading*. Boston: Allyn and Bacon.

Holdaway, D. 1979. *The foundations of literacy*. New York: Ashton Ed.

Jensen, E. 1996. *Brain-based learning*. Del Mar, CA: Turning Point Publishing.

Lusche, P. 2003. *No more letter of the week*. Peterborough, NH: Crystal Springs Books.

National Institute for Literacy. 2003. *Put reading first*. Washington, DC: National Institute for Literacy.

National Reading Panel. 2000. *Teaching children to read: An evidence-based assessment of the scientific research literature on reading and its implications for reading instruction*. Washington, DC: National Institute of Child Health and Human Development.

Scanlon, D. M., & Vellutino, F. R. 1996. Prerequisite skills, early instruction, and success in first grade reading: Selected results from a longitudinal study. *Mental Retardation and Developmental Disabilities Research Review*, 2, 54–63.

Schickedanz, J. 1999. *Much more than the ABCs*. Washington, DC: National Association for the Education of Young Children.

Schickedanz, J. & Casbergue, R. 2004. *Writing in preschool*. Newark, DE: International Reading Association.

Snow, C., Burns, M. S., & Griffin, P. 1998. *Preventing reading difficulties in young children*. Washington, DC: National Academy Press.

Stahl, S. 1992. Saying the "p" word: Nine exemplary guidelines for exemplary phonics instruction. *The Reading Teacher*, 45, 618–625.

Strickland, D. & Shanahan, T. 2004. Laying the groundwork for literacy. *Educational Leadership*, 3, 74–77.

Strickland, D. & Schickedanz, J. 2004. *Learning about print in preschool*. Newark, DE: International Reading Association.

Wolfe, P. & Nevills, P. 2004. *Building the reading brain, prek-3*. Thousand Oaks, CA: Corwin Press.

Wolf, M. 2007. *Proust and the squid*. New York: HarperCollins.

Letter Assessment Grid

Skill Development

Children will:

- develop alphabet recognition
- practice formative assessment

Use a grid similar to the one on this page to assess children's alphabet development throughout the school year. At the beginning of each month, ask the children to name all the uppercase and lowercase letters that they can. Fill in the letters with a different color each month for a visual overview of progress.

* Note: This assessment is intended as a supplement to other evaluations, checklists, and observational tools that you use.

Alphabet Assessment

Name

Month	Color	# of Letters
September	Red	
October	Orange	
November	Brown	
December	Yellow	
January	Blue	
February	Purple	
March	Green	
April	Pink	
May	Light Blue	

Research in Action

Children Develop Alphabetic Knowledge by:

- Playing with Letters
  - Literacy centers
  - Multi-sensory activities
  - Magnetic letters
  - Letter Collage (see page 77)
  - Letter games
- Linking Names of Letters and Sounds
  - Letter Wall (see page 45)
  - Name Games (see page 54)
  - ABC Books (see page 108)
  - Song: "Lettercise" (see page 70)
  - Sign Language (see page 55)
- Working with Rhymes and Language Games
  - Poetry club
  - Nursery rhyme songbook
  - Songs: "Hickety Pickety," "Yo Letters" (see pages 58, 71)
  - Rhyme Game (see page 56)
- Drawing and Writing Independently for Personal Enjoyment
  - Letter Lunchbox (see page 122)
  - Blank Books (see page 103)
  - Writing Center (see page 46)
  - Sign in
  - Invisible Writing (see page 95)
  - Rest and Doodle (see page 102)

Children Gain Print Knowledge by:

- Observing Adults as They Write
  - Morning Message (see page 17)
  - Sticky notes
  - Mystery person
- Contributing Ideas for Others to Write
  - Predictable books (I like…, I can…, I don't like…)
  - Dictate sentences about drawings
  - Journals (What I did today…)
  - Complete the sentence (language experience charts)
- Participating in Discussions About Labels and Signs
  - Read the room
  - Baggie Book (see page 107)
  - Box Tops (see page 25)
  - I Can Read! (see page 22)
  - Sweet ABCs
  - Lotto Match, Concentration (see page 59)

- Observing and Following Along as Adults Track Print
  - Letter Office (see page 45)
  - Pointers (see page 48)
  - Flashlight (see page 95)
  - Symbol story
- Independently Looking at Books, Drawing, and Writing
  - Collaborative books
  - Craft Stick Book (see page 105)
  - Pre-writing
  - Inviting library center (including lights, pillows, toys, puppets)

Children Practice Oral Language by:
- Creating Sounds by Singing and Making Music
  - Steady beat (paper towel rolls, paper plates, bodies)
  - Partner patty cake
  - Traditional games: "The Farmer in the Dell," "Ring Around the Rosie"
  - Copycat hand dance
- Listening and Responding to Music, Stories, and Discussions
  - Flannel board story
  - Circle story
  - Book talks
  - Tell and draw story
  - Dramatizations of rhymes and stories
- Listening for Various Purposes (enjoyment, to follow directions, engaging in dialogue, and attending to patterns)
  - Chants: "Alligator," "Chicka Chicka Boom Boom," "Boogaloo"
  - Fingerplays: "Heidi Hi and Louie Low" (see pages 17, 18, 31, 33)
  - Songs
  - Games: "Simon Says," "I Spy"
  - Fluency (shared reading, rereads, missing word)
  - Comprehension (Who? What? Where? When? Why?)
  - Magic Paintbrush (see page 74)
- Engaging in Oral Language Activities That Are Verbally Stimulating
  - Partner Share (see page 29)
  - Microphone (see page 29)
  - Tape recording studio/video
  - Rapid naming (categories game)

Favorite Traditional Rhymes for All Times

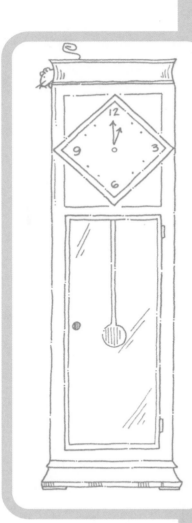

Diddle, Diddle, Dumpling
Diddle, diddle, dumpling,
My son John
Went to bed with his britches on.
One shoe off and one shoe on,
Diddle, diddle, dumpling,
My son John.

Hey, Diddle, Diddle
Hey, diddle, diddle,
The cat and the fiddle,
The cow jumped over the moon.
The little dog laughed.
To see such sport,
And the dish ran away
With the spoon.

Hickory Dickory Dock
Hickory, dickory, dock.
The mouse ran up the clock.
The clock struck one,
The mouse ran down.
Hickory, dickory, dock.

Humpty Dumpty
Humpty Dumpty sat on a wall.
Humpty Dumpty had a great fall.
All the king's horses,
And all the king's men,
Couldn't put Humpty
Together again.

Itsy Bitsy Spider
The itsy bitsy spider
Went up the waterspout.
Down came the rain and
Washed the spider out.
Out came the sun and
Dried up all the rain.
And the itsy bitsy spider
Went up the spout again.

Jack and Jill
Jack and Jill went up the hill
To fetch a pail of water.
Jack fell down and broke his
crown,
And Jill came tumbling after.

Jack Be Nimble
Jack be nimble.
Jack be quick.
Jack jump over
The candlestick.
Jump it lively.
Jump it quick.
But don't knock over
The candlestick!

Little Bo Peep
Little Bo Peep
Has lost her sheep
And can't tell where
To find them.
Leave them alone,
And they'll come home
Wagging their tails behind them.

Little Boy Blue
Little boy blue,
Come blow your horn.
The sheep's in the meadow,
The cow's in the corn.
Where is the boy
Who looks after the sheep?
Under the haystack fast asleep!

Little Jack Horner
Little Jack Horner
Sat in a corner
Eating his Christmas pie.
He stuck in his thumb,

And pulled out a plum,
And said,
"What a good boy am I!"

Little Miss Muffet
Little Miss Muffet
Sat on a tuffet,
Eating her curds and whey.
Along came a spider
And sat down beside her.
And frightened
Miss Muffet away!

Mary Had a Little Lamb
Mary had a little lamb,
Little lamb, little lamb.
Mary had a little lamb.
Its fleece was white as snow.

And everywhere that Mary went,
Mary went, Mary went.
And everywhere that Mary went
The lamb was sure to go.

It followed her to school one day,
School one day, school one day.
It followed her to school one day
Which was against the rule.

Mary, Mary, Quite Contrary
Mary, Mary, quite contrary,
How does your garden grow?
With silver bells and cockle shells
And pretty maids all in a row.

Old King Cole
Old King Cole was a merry old soul,
And a merry old soul was he.
He called for his pipe,
And he called for his bowl,
And he called for his fiddlers three.

Old Lady in the Shoe
There was an old lady
Who lived in a shoe.
She had so many children

She didn't know what to do.
She gave them some broth
Without any bread.
She hugged them all soundly
And sent them to bed.

Peas Porridge Hot
Peas porridge hot,
Peas porridge cold.
Peas porridge in the pot
Nine days old.

Some like it hot.
Some like it cold.
Some like it in the pot
Nine days old.

The Queen of Hearts
The queen of hearts
Made some tarts
All on a summer's day.
The knave of hearts
He stole those tarts
And took them clean away.

Rain, Rain, Go Away
Rain, rain, go away.
Come again another day.
All the children want to play.
Rain, rain, go away.

Ring Around a Rosie
Ring around a rosie
A pocketful of posies.
Upstairs, downstairs,
We all fall down.

Rock-a-Bye, Baby
Rock-a-bye, baby
In the treetop.
When the wind blows,
The cradle will rock.
When the bow breaks,
The cradle will fall,
And down will come baby
Cradle and all.

Sing a Song of Sixpence

Sing a song of sixpence
A pocket full of rye,
Four and twenty black birds
Baked in a pie.
When the pie was opened
The birds began to sing.
Now, wasn't that a dainty dish
To set before the king?

Three Little Kittens

The three little kittens,
They lost their mittens,
And they began to cry,
"Oh, mother dear, we sadly fear,
Our mittens we have lost."

"What, lost your mittens?
You naughty kittens!
Then you shall have no pie."
"Boo-hoo, boo-hoo,
We shall have no pie."

The three little kittens,
They found their mittens,
And they began to cry,
"Oh, mother dear, see here, see
    here,
Our mittens we have found."

"What, found your mittens,
You darling kittens!
Then you shall have some pie."
"Meow, meow,
We shall have some pie."

Twinkle, Twinkle, Little Star

Twinkle, twinkle, little star.
How I wonder what you are?
Up above the world so high,
Like a diamond in the sky.
Twinkle, twinkle, little star.
How I wonder what you are?

Wee Willie Winkie

Wee Willie Winkie
Runs through the town
Upstairs and downstairs
In his nightgown.
Tapping at the window
And crying through the lock,
"Are the children in their beds
For now it's eight o'clock?"

Additional Resources on the Internet

Websites

abc123kindergarten.com

abcteach.com

aslpro.com

atozteacherstuff.com

brainpop.com

busyteacherscafe

calicocookie.com

carlscorner.com

carlscorner.us

coolmath.com

crayola.com

disciplinehelp.com

dltk-teach.com

dolch-words.com

drjean.org

edhelper.com

educational press.com

enchantedlearning.com

eric-carle.com

everythingpreschool.com

farrm@aol.com

freeclipart.com

gigglepoetry.com

help4teachers.com

homestead.com

hubbardscupboard.org

hummingbirded.com

ilovekindergarten.com

innovativeclassroom.com

janbrett.com

jmeacham.com

jmeacham.com

kellyskindergarten.com

kidconcoctions.com

kinderart.com

kinderbykim.com

kinderfriends.com

kindergarten4thearts.com

kinderhive.com

kinderkorner.com

kinder-l@mail.cmsd.bc.ca
   (Canadian list serve)

kindernetonline.com

kinderpond.com

kizclub.com

krampf.com (science experiments)

lessonplanet.com

lessonplans.com

lindaslearninglinks.com

littlegiraffes.com

loveandlogic.com

makinglearningfun.com

marcias-lesson-links.com

members.shaw.ca/henriksent/
   index.htm

mrsalphabet.com

mrsdiminnie.com

mrsdiminnie.com

mrsmcgowan.com

mrspohlmeyerskinderpage.com

ncpe4me.com/energizers
   (brain breaks)

nuttinbutkids.com

ourschoolfamily.com

perpetualpreschool.com

pre-kpages.com

preschoolexpress.com

preschoolprintables.com

proteacher.com

puzzlemaker.com

readinga-z.com

readwritethink.org

sewhat4you.corp (teacher resources)

sharonmacdonald.com

signwithme.com

songsforteaching.com

starfall.com

storytellin.com

teacherhelpers.homestead.com

teachers.net
teachingheart.net
teachingisaworkofheart.com
teachingmadeeasier.com
technospud.com
thebestkidsbooksite.com
theideabox.com
thekcrew.net
thereadinglady.com
thereadinglady.com
theschoolbell.com
thevirtualvine.com
tinsnips.org
tlcart.com
tobey.ushaonline.net

Sites for Children and Parents
aplaceofourown.org
bemboszoo.com
billybear4kids.com
bobthebuilder.com
childfun.com
ed.gov/Family/RWN/Activ97/begin.
   html
familyfun.com
funbrain.com
funschool.com
jellybelly.com
kidfun.com
kidsdomain.com
nea.org
nncc.org
parentsoup.com
pbskids.org
smarterkids.com
smarterkids.com
yahooligans.com

Sites for Resource/Research
brainconnections.com
britannica.com
dictionary.com
edpubs.gov
encyclopedia.com
google.com
howstuffworks.com
infoplease.com
libraryspot.com
naeyc.org
nifl.gov
reading.org (ira)

Index